UGLY DUCKLING PRESSE :: DOSSIER

MOTION
STUDIES

JENA OSMAN

ISBN 978-1-946433-23-7
First Edition, First Printing, 2019
1000 copies

Dossier Series
Ugly Duckling Presse
The Old American Can Factory
232 Third Street #E303
Brooklyn, NY 11215
www.uglyducklingpresse.org

Distributed by
SPD/Small Press Distribution (USA)
Inpress Books (UK)
Raincoast Books via Coach House Books (Canada)

Cover art by Amze Emmons
Cover design by goodutopian
Typesetting by goodutopian and Sevendoubleyou
Typeset in Whitman, Benton Sans, and Franklin Gothic

Printed in the USA by McNaughton & Gunn
Cover stock from Mohawk Fine Papers Inc.

This book was made possible, in part, by the continued support
of the New York State Council on the Arts.

Contents

MOTION STUDIES

MOTION STUDIES

Air is the generosity of fog.
—Erin Mouré, *Little Theatres*

…the way a book can also be a repository of time…
—William Kentridge, *Secondhand Reading*

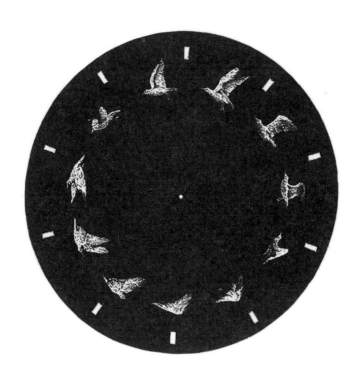

PART I: THE GRAPHIC METHOD

A small action sets off the ones to come. Someone finds a book in a library and is taken with the pictures. "Taken with," as if an image can take hold of you and move you along. In the corner of each page, at the end of each paragraph, an image slightly different from the last. As the pages turn, stillness becomes animate.

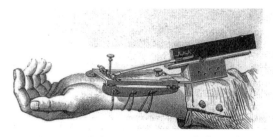

Sphygmograph device, Marey, *La méthode graphique*

The nineteenth-century physiologist Étienne-Jules Marey saw the body as a machine and wanted to understand its mechanics. He created a number of ingenious instruments in order to understand the rules of motion. His first well-known device, invented in 1859, was a graphing tool called a sphygmograph, which measured the rhythms of the blood as it moved through to the heart. An improvement on prototypes recently constructed in Germany, Marey's version was lighter, portable, and—most significantly—created a readable output. The analyst says come in, sit down.

The sphygmograph worked by pressing one part of a lever against the pulse in the wrist while the other part was connected to a stylus. The stylus traced the pressure of the blood in the artery onto a sheet of carbon. As the blood expanded the artery, the pen moved up; as the artery relaxed, the pen moved down. Reading the heart via the "graphic method" was a matter of translating a text of hills and valleys. I'm kind of nervous when I take tests, says the bird. The analyst says, Please don't move.

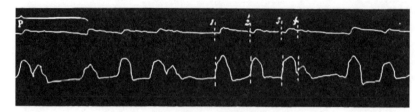

Irregular heartbeat, Marey, *Physiologie Expérimentale*

The device received a prize from the Académie des Sciences and Marey was invited to demonstrate its workings to Napoleon III. At the demonstration, all those present had the pattern of their blood drawn by the device; an irregularity was detected in one of the participants, who died a few days later. Marey's reputation was sealed. Reaction time is a factor in this, so please pay attention and answer as quickly as you can. Sure.

—·—

They had struck gold; they'd won the right to be forgotten. The ticket granted them that. All they had to do was sign on the dotted line and then disappear into the sunset, onto the horizon, around the corner, into the mist, over the rainbow, into complete silence.

But for their breath.

The noise of her pulse. Of his.

"The hellish tattoo of the heart" recorded in a line.

They draw a breath and it's made visible,
They have a thought and that's visible as well.

Shallow breath and stealth. Holding breath—

[to ward off the tracker]
[to escape the sensor][the reader]

—·—

Marey knew that every function of the human body, no matter how hidden in the folds, creates movement; he simply needed to find a way to transfer those movements to paper, turn them into data to be analyzed. Prior to the sphygmograph, a doctor would listen to the heart with a stethoscope, and then make determinations on what he perceived in the overheard pattern. The sphygmograph dispensed of that human intermediary. As the blood moved from one chamber to another, it was the pulse itself that caused the graphing machine to create a visual record more reliable, more stable than words. Is that part of the test? asks the bird.

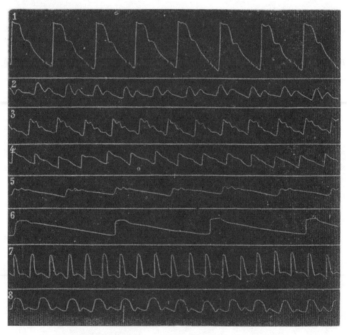

Sphygmograph readout, Marey, *La méthode graphique*

Repetitive peaks, oscillating hills, steep slopes, climbing waves, hooked points, horizontal summits, descending planes, flat valleys, dripping stalactites. No, says the analyst. Just warming you up, that's all.

An eye blinking becomes a landscape.

She sees him in his suit, in the clinic, sleeping.
The machine by the bed traces his breath and pulse.
The charted lines become an ultrasound.
The fetal shape becomes a shoulder of meat.
The shoulder of meat becomes a foot.
The foot becomes a heart.
The heart becomes a skull.
The skull becomes a face.
The eyes in the face are in the rear view mirror.
Rain hits the windshield.
The windshield wipers wave back and forth,
leave a trace of themselves from every position.

Post-procedure, he's now a transparent man who lives more as a trace, a clue, data. She is the same, though opaque. They run.

[tracker][reader][analyst][bird]

—•—

Decades later, Marey's graph of blood was replaced with a graph of voltage in time. In the electrocardiogram's conventional form, ten electrodes are placed on the arms, legs, and chest, and the heart's electricity is measured over a period of ten seconds. Electrodes detect electrical changes as the heart muscles depolarize when they beat. The readout in a typical heart is an orderly pattern. EKGs are now available in a wearable bio-sensor form, tracking heart rates, stress levels, fatigue, and mood. An algorithm translates the data into tips for positive change that appear on your hand-held device. You're in a desert, walking along in the sand when all of a sudden—Is this the test now? asks the bird.

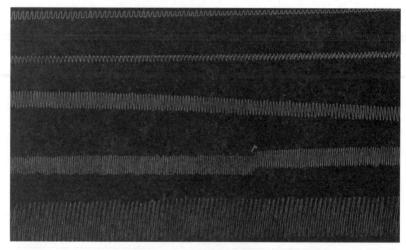

Polygraph readout/heartchart, Marey, *La méthode graphique*

To disappear beyond the company horizon. She knows a guide who can get them there. There is a tense meeting in a coffee shop, pre-screened for infrared sensors. The guide shows up in a teal tracksuit, conspicuous, with too many devices clipped to the waist.

As they listen to the plan, he can feel his heart start to race. She senses his flush, looks quickly to the guide to see if the flush is picked up, if transparency has been compromised. The guide (oblivious, or faking oblivion?) unfolds maps. Topographical lines in black, plum, and tangerine. This is the safest route in. This is the next best option. Special equipment might be needed.

Though he has been practicing stimuli resistance, he feels his brain emit a strong electrical surge, his fever pitch. Is the map, in fact, a probe? Has their position been detected and registered?

The guide explains the topographical key: Black for flat valleys, plum for steep slopes, tangerine for peaks. Not recommended for solo travel. Does she have a partner?

—•—

The nineteenth century was crowded with graphing machines, all of which provided a sense of life as a continuum, rather than a set of stills. Cardiographs drew the heart, thermographs drew heat, pneumographs drew the breath, myographs drew muscle movements. Polygraphs drew it all together. What desert? asks the bird.

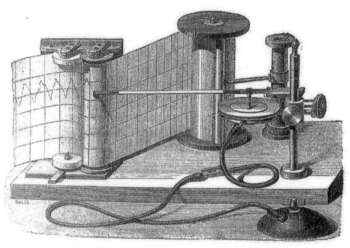

Polygraph machine, Marey, *La méthode graphique*

The polygraph as lie detector is a familiar crime story device. Picture the accused hooked up with wires to a machine, the stern voice of the interrogator, a needle drawing peaks and valleys, measuring veracity. The lie detector tracks the twitches and responses with a graph; it draws the body under stress. Its efficacy is dependent upon a belief that lying creates a predictable physiological response, distinct from when the body tells the truth. Doesn't make any difference what desert, it's completely hypothetical, says that analyst.

The guide hands her a pair of glasses that provide a promotional hologram of what is on offer. She takes it in; he keeps his eyes on the guide. Although translucent and unseen, he tries to relax his jaw, knowing that when the jaw isn't relaxed, what is produced is a visible tell.

She sees hills in the background and crags laden with ripening grapes. She sees Poseidon motioning for her to come closer, then much closer, whispering in her ear about raw force and new energy and abundance.

She sets the glasses down on the table and tries to relax her jaw. She keeps her eyes on the guide as the terms of the transaction are explained. Transport into safe untraceable space, beyond street view, New Wilderness—on the condition that she wear a wrist-watch device.

His inner body screams at the contradiction: disappearance, but only while uploading data? The hydraulics of his circulatory engine switch into overdrive. Vital force. The flush starts to spread like a poison, preparing to give him away, the folded corner of a page. He needs to slow his respiratory rate, thin the blood volume, slow the pulse, calm the skin to flat transparency.

—·—

The connection between vital signs and the articulation of truths was eventually proved unreliable. In the 1998 case *United States v. Scheffer*, the Supreme Court determined that the polygraph yielded information no better than an opinion. However, the U.S. Department of Defense continued to believe. In 2008 in Afghanistan, it made use of the Preliminary Credibility Assessment Screening System, which consists of a computer connected by a USB cable to a black wrist cuff. Electrodes are attached to the fingertips with Velcro to measure sweat, and a wire measures the pulse. A series of questions are asked. Green indicates truth, red indicates deception, yellow indicates uncertainty. Do you make up these questions? asks the bird. Or do they write them down for you?

Are the lights on in this room?

Are you now sitting down?

Did you ever make a promise that you had no intention of keeping?

Did you participate in placing that bomb near that road?

Did you ever lie to take advantage of a friendship?

Did you ever blame someone for something you did?

Did you place that bomb near the road?

Did you ever bring shame upon yourself or your family?

—·—

The "wristwatch device" is actually an implant that has an exterior band made to look like a vintage timepiece, a dash of magazine fashion. The guide explains how it's programmed to transmit bio-sensory information, like heart rate, medical needs, sleep patterns. "It will be your guardian, protector. It will bring good things to you."

He had argued with her before the implant procedure. She saw him grab her wrist, but upon contact, the outlines of his hand melted away; she felt nothing. In an earlier moment in her life, she might have described him as a ghost, a spiritual manifestation of the past. But she knows better now; invisibility is a prison. "Haunting" is a quaint and faint manifestation of the tortured.

He had ranted about privacy rights, as if they could exist anymore. The idea of them as old-fashioned as the fake watch-face now sealed to her wrist. She knew there was just one way forward and she understood the cost: the facts of her interior, available for use in a public dataset, as part of some kind of game. Besides, she hadn't made a fuss when he underwent his own erasure.

"Yes, I am a pawn. Can we please go now?"

———

Quantimetric self-tracking, biometric collection, the uploading and gamification of a body: one could say that Marey's sphygmograph was the precursor to any number of self-monitoring devices that measure the body's interior state and turn the data into a graphic visualization. Skin temperature, galvanic skin response, steps taken, stairs climbed, distance traveled, calories burned, sleep quality, heart rate, steps taken, calories burned, eating habits, sleep quality and sleep cycle, water consumption, movement, steps taken, calories burned, distance traveled, calories burned, motion, sleep tracking, body temperature, steps taken, heart rate, calorie consumption, number of hours of light and deep sleep, period and fertility tracking, steps taken, mood and energy, alcohol intake, work/life time tracking, blood pressure, body scale, body mass index, pulse. The analyst proposes the first question: the tortoise lays on its back, its belly baking in the hot sun.

Lume. Lark.
Clue. Glow.
Mood. Nudge.
Tictrac. Gomore.
Pebble. Heartmath.
Withings. Simband.
Jawbone. Misfit.
Sleep as Android. MyFitnessPal.
QardioBase. IMeasureU.

SleepBot. WakeMate.
Zeo. Beddit.
Cooey. WellBee.
Lifeband Touch.
Fitbit Flex.
Apple Watch.
Ultrathin.
Kindara.
Runtastic.

Garmin Vivoactive.
Zephyr BioHarness.

—•—

A line writes itself on the table.

He knows that arguing is useless.

It runs and flows across the screen.

He has to let go of his anxiety and trust her.

From one window to the next.

He knows if he asks a question, she will reply truthfully.

There's an empty town square with a fountain.

She would never make a promise she had no intention of keeping.

Eventually the room becomes writing.

He knows she will never tell a lie to take advantage of his friendship, or his compromised state of being.

The line goes from one window in the square to the next.

If he asks her to push the button, pull the trigger, sound the alarm, she will do so.

The city breathes in linear curves of cursive and data glow.

The lights are on in this room. They are now sitting down. This might be the last conversation they will ever have out loud.

"Yes, of course, let's go."

—·—

Measuring cardiac movement was just the beginning for Marey; he soon turned his attention to the movement of muscle in both humans and animals. He invented "experimental shoes" that tracked the pressure of footfalls and their duration. A long tube ran from a small air chamber in the shoe's rubber sole to a drum and stylus held by the subject. But you're not helping, continues the analyst.

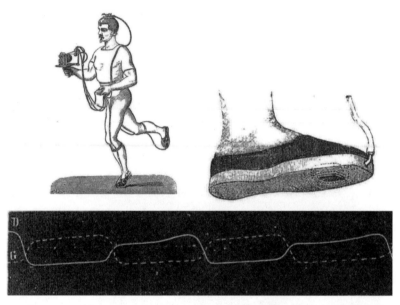

Experimental lever drum and shoe, Marey, *Animal Mechanism*; Tracings of an ordinary walk, Marey, *Animal Mechanism*

We see that the pressure of the right (droit) begins when the left (gauche) decreases. An alternation of impacts that measures time, not space, on a cylinder of carbon. What do you mean I'm not helping, says the bird, getting angry.

Similarly, a horse's gait was measured with the help of another special shoe. This time a ball of India-rubber filled with horsehair was attached to the hoof. When the foot hit the ground, the ball was compressed, and air pushed through the transmission tube to the inscribing apparatus. The method didn't work so well on regular roads (the ball was quickly destroyed), so Marey came up with another solution—a kind of leather bracelet fastened above the ankle. I mean you're not helping, says the analyst. Why is that?

Trotting horse with experimental instruments, Marey, *Animal Mechanism*

The rider held the registering instrument and collected the graphic signals; Marey called these "synoptical notations." Each bar was a rhythm marker, the length corresponding with duration. The rhythm of an amble is different from the rhythm of a trot or a gallop. It was a score to be read by the analyzing reader. The bird is silent, perhaps panicking. How can a bird pass this test?

Although the guide had claimed that the wristwatch was for emergencies, tracking location and life signs in case the New Wilderness turned treacherous and an extraction was required, they assume it is also a listening device. They need a silent language, so they start by writing notes. The device is on her right wrist. She trains herself to write with her left hand so her movements can't be transcribed.

They wait for the delivery of supplies.

The delivery man is from South America and undocumented, a contractor for a multi-national goods supplier. He knows the routine. He bips the barcode, which is then uploaded, location registered. A GPS satellite tells him where to go in his silver Astrovan. He rings the door buzzer, which connects to the customer's cell phone, and is buzzed in. He drops the package in the mail room, humming with radio frequencies, and bips the barcode again. While the customer is getting ready to upload his review of goji berries harvested in Brazil, he consults his map app for the next address. "Laser Delivery" is written on his van in black electrical tape.

She sees the van pull up. The buzzer disrupts with a loud alarm. After a moment of hesitation, she picks up her phone and says hello. A gruff voice says "package downstairs" and hangs up.

Ankle bracelets were first used by the United States criminal justice system in 1983. Assigned primarily to wealthy offenders as a prison alternative at the start, they are now frequently required as part of parole agreements, for juvenile truants, and for immigrants waiting for their asylum cases or deportation hearings to begin. Not an alternative, but an extension and expansion. The monitoring device consists of a black plastic bracelet and an electronic box that's linked to a phone line 24 hours a day. Some work via radio frequency (RF), and some track location via global positioning (GPS). You are free to move about the building while a constellation of satellites tracked by the Air Force tunes into your frequencies. You are free to move outside the building to a pre-approved list of sites—denied the chance encounter, the yard sale, the conversation on the street with a neighbor. The police and/or the probation officer hold the registering instrument and collect the signals. When the signal is broken, they move in and make an arrest—not for a crime that endangers public safety, but for breaking the rules of the device. The suspicious computer and voice imprint, continuous receiving centers, demand the best from your house arrest. The companies that "lease" the equipment often charge a fee; a prisoner may owe thousands for the equipment needed to continue their home detention. A leash instead of a cage. A tether. A homing device. An open-air prison. Absolute location is the world moving around you. A body with a monitor enters a store; another body with a monitor enters the same store. Is trouble brewing, or do they both need to buy toothpaste? Can the device interpret the world? They're just questions, says the analyst. It's a test designed to provoke an emotional response. Shall we continue? The bird nods yes.

—

A line drawn becomes a field

He opens the suitcase
His former body bleeds out
Newspaper pages blow over it
Then fly off

Before the mirror
His face replaced by a tub of blue water

His face replaced by hers
Looking back at him and through

[reader][tracker][characters][birds]

In order to understand the flight of birds, Marey created a myographic bird harness. A pigeon was fitted with a corset. Wedged tightly between the corset and the bird's pectoral muscles was a small metal pan with a spiral spring. Long transmitting tubes connected the pan with the recording drum. The bird's muscles produced an undulating trace on the smoked surface of a cylinder. An ascending curve for contractions, a descending curve for relaxations. It seems you don't think our work is of benefit to the public, says the bird to the analyst.

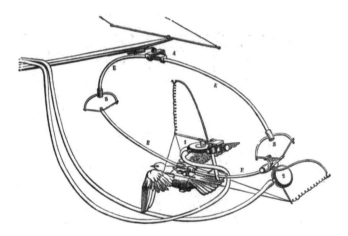

Bird harness, Marey, *Animal Mechanism*

In an improved version, the bird harness used threads of twisted silk attached to the wings. The bird moved with the apparatus rather than having to carry it. Three levers inscribed the multi-dimensions of flight on the cylinder. The transcribed output was like an acoustical wave of repeating hills and valleys. You're either a benefit or a hazard; if you're a benefit, then it's not my problem, says the analyst.

After opening the delivery and packing their bags, she tosses her phone. They set out without words. She tries to remember how they felt just a week before, pulling the ticket, elated that their records would be scratched clean and shredded. There were many records. At first this seemed a good thing, a way to share their life with the world. But with each failure to participate in the system, they had to register their failure with the company. Loan documents. Medical bills. Run-ins with the law while trying to catch up. Each room they visited recorded their presence and submitted their profiles to an algorithm. Each object they carried reported a radio wave in air. Each piece of paper took all of their information and each corner of every room charged their outlines with infrared. Even in his trace state, they compiled him for their records. And with each data extraction, the body bled further out.

It was a miracle they had been set free by lottery.

She recognizes the wristwatch as a shackle, but believes that he has sacrificed even more.

They wear typical tourist garb, although his is not apparent. Sunglasses, comfortable footwear, backpacks.

The words "off the grid" fill the ad spaces throughout the subway car. It is marketing for a popular lifestyle brand. The slogan sells a fantasy, much like that of the privacy profiteers. Nonetheless, they plan to breach the fantasy's borders.

—·—

Objects can communicate with each other, thanks to radio frequency identification tags. Once a tag/transponder is attached to an object (or hidden within it), it's ready to transfer its entire history to a reader. It's an embedded sleeper cell waiting to be awakened. In clothing, in luggage, in passports, credit cards, on container ships, in cattle—all it wants to do is to send its information payload through the oscillating waves to the machine receiver. The reader energizes the tag, the mesmerizing signal curve. Object to object, reporting on the subject. Skimming and eavesdropping. The bird doesn't even know its movements are being studied. Is this to be an empathy test? asks the bird. Capillary dilation of the so-called blush response? Fluctuation of the pupil? Involuntary dilation of the iris?

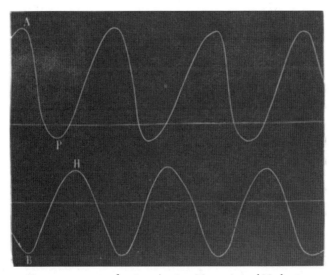

Trace movements of a pigeon's wing, Marey, *Animal Mechanism*

Marey knew that ultimately his graphic method was falling short. It required a physical connection between the measuring instrument and the subject at hand; for example, the bird on a tether. Was the bird really free? Wasn't the harness interfering with the natural movements of the bird? Though the physical contact required by the graphic method was certainly less deadly, was it so different from the cuts of the vivisectionists? Was there a way to measure motion with zero impact? Alright, I'm going to ask you a series of questions, says the analyst. Just relax and answer them as simply as you can.

———•———

They take the bus to the end of the line. Perhaps someone notices her, a tourist, scribbling awkwardly in her notebook with her left hand. Trying to be inconspicuous as she rests the notepad on her knee and looks sideways at the empty seat beside her.

As she moves her body, air currents displace. They push against his outline.

It is a slow and careful conversation, due to the tedium of the left hand. They will have to find a better way. They try blinking. They try facial expressions. They try some rudimentary signing. Ultimately they will need to rely on their intuition and understanding of one another.

She keeps catching herself about to use her right hand as they communicate, grimaces. He writes in the notebook "I could break that arm for you" and she laughs. Perhaps someone notices a woman alone on a bus laughing to herself.

She is aware that less than 24 hours since implant, the skin around the device is beginning to fester. She pulls the sleeve of her sweater further down so that he can't see. They are almost there.

PART II: CHRONOPHOTOGRAPHY

It's not the retina, but the mind. Someone finds an image in a maga-zine and writes a letter. A letter resists 24 frames per second. In the corner of each page, at the end of each paragraph, an image slight-ly different, producing motion. The thumb controls the pace of the pages turning. Between each still, a gutter for acts of animation.

Étienne Jules Marey and Eadweard James Muybridge shared initials. They came into the world and left it within weeks of one another. A line flies out of one window and into another, threading them together. Their timelines crossed when Leland Stanford, for-mer governor of California and railroad entrepreneur, read Marey's book *Animal Mechanism* in 1874. Stanford, in an attempt to recover from the labors of building a transcontinental rail system, had taken an interest in racehorses. In his quest to own the fastest horses on earth, he was heavily invested in resolving the question of "unsup-ported transit": was there a moment during a gallop when all four of a horse's legs are in the air, when the horse could be said to have taken flight? The human eye was too slow to answer. Stanford hired Muybridge (who had made his reputation photographing the Amer-ican West) to capture an image of a horse with all of its feet sus-pended in the course of a run, and to lay this question to rest once and for all. At first, Muybridge argued that such a photograph was not possible—shutter speed could never be quick enough to capture the phenomenon. After Stanford read Marey's book, he instructed Muybridge to shift his approach from a single shot to a sequence. There was a delay, as Muybridge had to skip town after killing his wife's lover, but he took up the photographic research again (with Stanford's continuing patronage) in 1877. Thus in 1878, a California crowd gathered. Muybridge lined up twelve cameras in a row, with twelve wires running across the track. As the horse flew by, with a white screen as backdrop, the snapped wires triggered the shutters in a rolling percussion, and the question was finally answered in se-ries. Now it's the security guard and the bird.

—·—

They sit at a rest stop picnic table and unfold the topographical maps while eating sandwiches. He surveys the area, the flat valley of the parking lot, and registers the camera locations. In his notebook he makes mathematical notations, looking for gaps in the camera sightlines. He locates a narrow path they can take.

She indicates she'll be back and heads to the mini-mart. On the way to the bathroom, she buys some chewing gum and anti-bacterial ointment. She can see herself on the black and white TV screen behind the cashier, waiting in line while a tall, burly man buys a tank of gas, a pack of cigarettes, and an energy drink with his credit card. The transaction registers his location, his purchases are subjected to an algorithm; is this a recognizable purchasing pattern for the burly man? As he leaves the store, and unknown to him, he lands in a picture taken by a teenager that gets uploaded to social media and dispersed to many followers. The face is then added to a database of faces. While rounding the corner of the mini-mart, a wine-dark dome above his head tracks his moves.

She pays with cash.

—•—

In 1878, the French science journal *La Nature* published photo-engraved reproductions (etched heliographs) of Muybridge's horse photos. Marey was stunned by the images—they proved that the long and awkward photographic process had become instantaneous—and he immediately wrote a letter to the editor. Addressed to Muybridge, the letter urged him to apply his methods to birds in flight, and mentioned Marey's own personal dream of a photographic gun. The security guard's ears perk up; he's got 1500 cameras.

Muybridge was perhaps more artist than scientist (though he filed patents for many inventions). Thanks to a European tour funded by Stanford, he showed up in Paris in 1881, ready to entertain and amaze. His magic lantern show consisted of a modified zoetrope—a "zoopraxiscope"—which projected images of trotting horses and birds in flight onto a screen. In order to project his photographs without distortion, Muybridge redrew them and had stretched them out. The guard informs the bird: of the 1500 cameras, he has 720 on the hotel side, quadruple redundancy on the gaming floor.

While Muybridge's photos were enjoyed by many, they didn't satisfy Marey's scientific curiosity. The sequences were manually arranged, a constructed illusion more than a true depiction of movement in time. What are we looking for, and where do we start? asks the bird. You tell me, says the guard.

—•—

In the bathroom stall she turns her shirt inside out, from black to plum. She ties a scarf around her hair. She inspects the festering at her wrist and applies the ointment, wondering if she will need antibiotics. That would be an enormous setback, requiring ID, health insurance, tests, prescriptions—too many breadcrumbs to count.

She chews a piece of the gum. Out of the stall, she uses the gum to affix a note beneath the sink: "I was here." Before she can retract this nonsensical gesture, a woman comes in, so she studiously washes her hands. The woman is texting, typing words that travel via satellite to her mother three states away. Each data bit is translated into code, then reconstituted into English as it hits its intended target. The moment in between is a gutter between frames where everything happens.

She thinks that if she were the hunter, she'd have a gun in her purse. But she is not the hunter.

She walks back through the mini-mart, aware that the camera is recording her from above. The lens behind the register passes her image on to the dome above the door and so on.

—·—

In 1873, astronomer Pierre-César Jules Janssen invented a photographic "revolver" in order to record the planet Venus as it crossed the circle of the sun. A sensitized plate rotated at 70 second intervals and took a series of impressions arranged in a circle, showing the planet's progress. When Muybridge failed to capture the flight of birds, Marey set to work, as was his way, on improving Janssen's device. He transformed the revolver (which was more of a floor-model cannon than a gun) into a portable rifle-shaped camera. It was 10 times faster than Janssen's revolver, and you could hitch it on your shoulder like a hunter of birds. The guard punches up camera 383 and homes in on the guy in the checkered shirt.

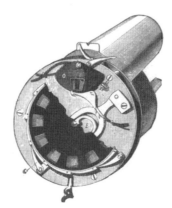

Photographic gun, Marey, *Movement*

When the trigger was pulled, the plate turned twelve times per second, creating a sequence of 12 images. The instrument was quite precise, capturing the sequence of flight in a way that matched space with time. Unlike the graphic method, which could provide only a scriptive trace of movement, the photographic method captured movement and form simultaneously, without interference. There was no more need for tubes and harnesses—all that was required was light. Boss, I think we got another hooker in the Princess Lounge, says the guard in series, Let's punch up 596. The bird says, Excuse me a second, and runs down the stairs.

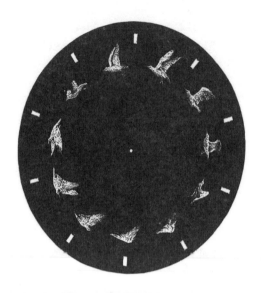

Image taken with the photographic gun, Marey, *Le Vol des Oiseaux*

While she was in the mini-mart, he had moved to a different picnic table, close to the wooded edge of the rest area, near the narrow path. She knows that one minute she will be visible on screen, and the next she will be gone, like a magic trick. Will this constitute a problematic pattern? Will video analytics pick it up and trigger an alarm? That is the risk.

He raises his eyebrows as if to say *Ready?* She nods yes.

The narrow path takes them to a barbed-wire fence. There is an opening, a metal gash, just as the guide had said there would be. The safest route in. The path becomes a cascade of rocks on the side of a mountain in the falling dusk. Some of the rocks are slick with mist and there are moments of slide and stumble. Plum for steep slopes. They walk into the increasing dark, looking to the sky for light.

The only sound is their breath as they work their way up the mountain, hoping to make it above treeline before it's too dark to see. She feels her heart rate like gulping swallows down to the wristwatch, centrifugal twister, like an energy leaving her. A leap through the solar system to the monitor on earth. Again and again like that.

—•—

Closed circuit TV was created during WWII by German engineer Walter Bruch in order to monitor V-2 rocket launchers from a safe distance. There was no recording apparatus, just a direct live broadcast from event to screen. In 1969, nurse Marie Van Brittan Brown, and her electronics technician husband, Albert, patented the first CCTV home security system. The patent drawings depict someone in bed looking at a TV screen that shows a visitor at the front door. The image of the visitor was captured by a camera behind a peephole, which then fed the image to the monitor via a radio-controlled wireless system. The person in the bed could talk to the visitor, buzz them in, or contact the police—but as with the Bruch system, nothing was recorded. The monitor had to be a live person watching the screen. Variations of this system were quickly adopted by apartment buildings everywhere. The guard in series says to the bird, Come on, grab a radio, stay on channel three.

Eventually, the invention leapt from the monitoring of private space to surveilling public space, all in the name of security. A bank of monitors, with a single guard (a "force multiplier"). Fixed and pan-tilt cameras with 30x zoom lenses, controlled with a joystick and a keyboard. Images recorded on videotapes or DVR. In the 1990s, digital technology made it easier to record and store images, which led to a rapid increase in the use of the cameras. To save storage space, only one of every six seconds are recorded, a stuttering recounting. Half a century after the Browns' patent, millions of CCTVs, connected via satellite, scan various populations across the world as they go about their business. Whether in a small town or a big city, your image is caught on camera throughout the day. The guard recalls "The Zero Gravity Flying Eye"; it floated all over the arena to get crowd reaction. Let me see its tape, says the bird, with dread.

Notice. Security cameras in use. This facility may be protected by video surveillance. For your protection you are being videotaped. Security notice. This property is protected by video surveillance: Trespassers will be prosecuted. Security cameras and audio devices are recording persons and activity. Video surveillance in use on these premises. Warning. This property under video surveillance. No trespassing. Monitored by video camera. You are being videotaped.

Premises protected by 24-hour audio & video surveillance. By entering you agree to be recorded. The guard scans the screens: "Now where is your girl?"

———•———

He tries to curl around her to keep her warm, but instead his out-line blends into hers like a thin veil. After the cold sleepless night above the trees, they watch the sky get lighter. They are in the tan-gerine peaks, eating energy bars and sipping from their canteens. The topographical map is spread out on the rock before them, its corners held down by smaller stones.

They are on a mountaintop. They know their destination is sup-posed to be hilly, not mountainous, and covered in grapevines. There are no vines in sight. They aren't sure how to get from here to there. How to jump into the space between stanzas, into the space between frames?

Meanwhile, signals transmit from her wrist, the data monitored and analyzed by a listening station, then passed on to intelligence services.

Suddenly there's a helicopter. They duck down to stay clear of the blades and don't know whether to run. The guide hadn't mentioned this part. Before they can think, someone leans out of the helicop-ter door with a rifle cocked, aims, shoots. She falls.

Suddenly there's a hunter. They duck down so as not to be seen and don't know whether to run. The guide hadn't mentioned this part. Before they can think, the hunter lifts his bow and arrow, aims, shoots. She falls.

Suddenly there's a storm. They pack up their things and start to move back toward the trees, but the rain makes it difficult to run. The guide hadn't mentioned this part. Before they get far, lightning lights, aims, strikes. She falls.

———

While funds for more surveillance cameras are often won by arguing that the technology reduces crime, the argument remains speculative. Meanwhile, the dream of threat prediction becomes more concrete: if there could be an uninterrupted view, if ominous patterns could be made visible, if the cameras could be linked, if the gaps could be closed and the sequence kept intact… If only it were possible to track a person the way we track a package, through a building, down a street, at a protest, in a car. They're near the lobby elevators. Change of plans. They're at the elevator. Take a right, the guard directs. The bird takes a right.

Governments and law enforcement hope for and work on total information systems. Dumb cameras are made smart, with software to sift through all the data. Facial recognition software scans the crowd. Cameras with microphones pick up conversations. License plate numbers are collected. Facelt. Visionics. Identix. Echelon. Trapwire. Situational awareness, counter-terrorism tech, swarm intelligence. Vulnerability assessment, predictive software, threat meters. Video content analysis categorizes images and tracks the patterns. It's old news by now. It's called the first draft of history, says the security guard in series. It's going to hold.

Of course there are problems. Poor image quality, not good enough to use in court. Lots of false positives when identifying faces. And the fact that the cameras are not yet networked; movement can't be traced in a continuous flow. Instead, there's a stop action fragmentation, a space between frames, a gutter between panels, a possible pivot between images. Too much narrative integrity lost to the blank. At least you got to be on TV, the guard jokes.

Marey's graphic method allowed a continuous tracking of the bird as it moved—but its movements were hindered by the measuring apparatus. His photographic gun set the bird free, but he was left with discrete units on glass. Is a threat like a bird on glass? Somehow the optical trace had to be ongoing so he could measure it all. Continuous motion capture. You hit the jackpot here, proclaims the guard in series. All you have to do is cash in your ticket.

When he sees her there on the ground, the worldline tilts.

Lights of a constellation in space
A sea of points connected by a dash, a gash
Dotted lines stitch the earth together
And the sound of electrical crickets

A fly on a revolving disk
An airplane creature
Stretched and distorted on the anamorphic plate,
But perfectly proportioned in reflection

Trees and rain and hawks,
A face, a goat, a carousel
Gas mask head on radio tower legs
The bird on a tether, a journey—

[to the sun][to the screen][to the stars]

In the early 1880s in France, physical education became a requirement for all students. The government wanted its citizens to have fortitude in the face of future conflicts. Gymnastic societies proliferated, all in the quest to reinvigorate the human muscles of the land. The bird, reduced to a system of bright lines, becomes a troupe of tap dancing penguins in Antarctica.

Marey was named Professor of Natural History of Organized Bodies at the Collège de France and given land in the Bois de Boulogne, where he built a laboratory to further investigate the muscular potential of men and animals. The Ministry of War had hopes that his research would reveal how to train a better soldier, how to march a stronger step, how to stave off fatigue. The bird, reduced to a system of bright lines, becomes a stingy, unfeeling and miserable man who has a change of heart.

As with his prior experiments, Marey was more interested in movement and the instruments that could help him measure it than in practical application. Marey's assistant, Georges Demeny (who also ran a school called the Circle for Rational Gymnastics), took care of the applied side of Marey's endeavors, and served as liaison between the lab and the world. The bird, reduced to a system of bright lines, becomes a trash-talking teddy bear.

It was during this period that Marey developed chronophotography. Frustrated by the partial and stuttered views produced by the photographic rifle, he invented a camera that could capture all of the phases of a movement, without gaps, on a single plate. Thanks to a rotating fenestrated metal disk behind an open lens, each step in a subject's progression would layer up against the previous one. The body multiplied in a true arc of movement unfolding in time. But as the disk turned faster, as the exposures got shorter, and as the images got sharper, the output started to blur and superimpose. There was too much information; the mechanics of movement couldn't express themselves legibly. The bird, reduced to a system of bright lines, becomes a slithering dragon.

Demeny walking, Marey, Collège de France archive

Marey responded to this problem by taking "partial" photographs, where the amount of information captured was greatly reduced. He covered the subject in black from head to foot, and marked the joints in white, or with metal buttons, or later with tiny lights. Thin white bands connected the dots. When the subject moved against a black background, the light and the camera picked up only the skeletal residue; the body was transformed into its own trace, a graphical notation. Marey named this method of motion capture "geometrical chronophotography." The bird, reduced to a system of bright lines, becomes a tavern owner with goggle glasses and a mysterious past.

 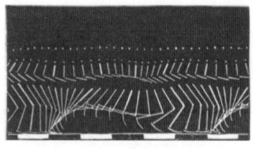

Man dressed in black, Marey, *Movement*; Runner reduced to a system of bright lines, Marey, *Movement*

Understanding the mechanics of the body required getting rid of the body. Thus, a body reduced and transformed to points and lines in a system of flow. A body drawing its own trajectory, its own output. According to Marey, chronophotographs could teach best practices (for athletes, for workers) better than any live demonstration, as they were capable of slowing time. A walk, a march, a jump, could be broken into small constituent parts for analysis. The thumb controls the pace of the pages. The army revised its training manuals and the government created a national physical education curriculum based on the information the chronophotographs revealed. The bird, reduced to a system of bright lines, becomes a legendary warrior who must slay a hideous creature.

—·—

Her body is lifted onto a stretcher for transport, and he clings to her, unseen, like mist. He feels hands move through him to secure her arms and legs, and to silently check her wristwatch device. He tries to keep his breath as quiet and even as possible, but fears his increased heart rate will sound an alarm.

How did they get caught in this net? They had been solid citizens at the company. When interest-targeted for purchases or events, they had purchased, they had attended. When asked to review, they had done so eagerly. They rated products, reviewed experiences, created wish lists. They left the RF tags in their clothing. At protests and demonstrations, they smiled for the police and their cameras. They fed all of their social media feeds. They had dabbled in online revelations and had uploaded video documentation. They had fed the machine so the broker would have plenty to sell. They had been sincere in their efforts. They had been efficient and true to their community. They each had recently received "employee of the month" program loyalty gift cards.

But somehow it had all gone awry. They had tried to keep coherent, but they kept falling apart, and the company had evidence in its archives. Their data profiles sent mixed signals, inputs were tagged as possible bots. At first each had tried to hide it from the other, ashamed of their algorithmic failure, anxious for their financial future. Until one night they confided in each other, surprised but relieved that they weren't alone in their honest mistakes. They strategized about how to clean up their data streams, their paradoxical profiles, their illegible patterning and unmarketable traces.

Now he can feel her heart beating, tucked beneath his own. He tries to get a sense of where they're going, what will happen to them. Then a black sheet is draped over her and all goes dark.

—·—

Motion capture was first used in biomechanical research in the 1970s, but was quickly recognized as a powerful tool for animators. In a motion capture studio, similar to the subjects in Marey's geometric chronophotographs, actors wear tight-fitting body suits with white reflective markers placed at the joints. Instead of Marey's bulky camera apparatus with its heavy glass disks, variously positioned digital cameras record the white markers 120 times or more per second, sending thousands of floating point values into a data file. The data files show the position and rotation of the body, but not its muscles or identity; the actor has been stripped away, leaving only movement behind. Extracted (ghosted) action is then used as a foundation for a virtual composition. In this way, animators create plausible human-like movements for their technicolor action heroes. Fight specialists don black skin-tight suits, with ping-pong balls Velcroed at the joints for video games like Total War and Splinter Cell. Cameras map their digital skeletons and track every move, render their forms on screen. Their human actions are captured, cleaned up, and skinned in the solve edit. The bird becomes a cursed captain with a tentacled face looking for souls to join him.

In order for the virtual to feel real, the real must be stripped of its body, dematerialized until just a dot or a line on screen remains. Then given a new skin. The bird becomes a long-headed yellow-eyed beast who says, "I smell you, I hear your breath."

Stereoscopic trajectory of a brilliant point placed at the level of the lumbar verte-
brae of a man walking away from the photographic camera, Marey, *Movement*

All he can hear is an engine. And then the engine stops. And then they are lifted from an interior to an exterior. And then the engine starts again without them. And then it is silent. He waits a long time. If he moves, if he lifts the black sheet and they aren't alone, his presence will be given away. He can still feel her heart beating against his, but slower, in a deep sleep. He wishes he could move through her, but he is only a transparent skin.

Eventually she twitches awake, unharmed. She throws the sheet, and him, off. He quickly looks around: lush grape arbors, rolling hills, not much else. Have they made it to New Wilderness? She looks down at her wrist and sees that the inflammation is gone. Her body feels sore. She thought she had died. There is a moment of wonder and relief.

But something is wrong. When they turn away from each other's eyes to the place that they're in, the arbor has become a barren tract of lines and objects, abandoned engineering projects, pipes, a culvert. Then the world begins to erase itself, then redraws back to the wild, only to disperse and decay again. They hold onto each other as if the earth might crack open, but nothing rumbles, nothing shakes. Just the smooth glide and reshuffle of competing landscapes. The barren tract erases, redraws, becomes the New Wilderness. Then the ghost of the former grows and embeds in the new. Then the new leaves its residue in the former, grapes scattered across a plot of dirt.

Is this a glitch?

Ghostcatching was a 1999 collaboration between dancer/choreographer Bill T. Jones and digital artists Shelley Eshkar and Paul Kaiser. Jones, with sensors attached to his joints and limbs, improvised before the cameras. Software tracked and captured his movements, his self reduced to dots. His body spun and lost its mass, its identity. A human animation tool took the skeleton of Jones' movement and mapped it onto a kinematic biped, a three dimensional figure that looked hand-drawn. A computer modeled applied geometry. For a time, the figure is contained within a sketched box (a phone booth? a coffin?), struggles to move inside of it, but ultimately breaks free. A captured movement trying to escape its capture. Each gesture leaves a mark, a chalk line, until the entire world of the piece is filled with the inscription of motion's residue. The sound of chalk drawn on a blackboard. Position. Rotation. A body draws a line in space, now a visible trace. The visible trace draws itself another body, a half-life of lines and planes and curves. The bird, reduced to a system of bright lines, becomes the chieftain of a Martian clan.

Reading the heart is a matter of understanding the variation of curves. Captured then breaking free again and again. With motion capture no one is there, but there's someone there. The ghost of each movement continuing as a visible chalked trace, the chalky streaked air. In analyzing pure motion, the body is lost. Yet, as Jones himself once stated, motion capture may be the best way to archive his life's work. The bird, reduced to a system of bright lines, becomes a big blue alien from the planet Pandora.

The ground beneath them shifts.

A man drinks coffee in another time and place.

The grapevines break into the earth.

Pages of his book show a moon in the sky.

The earth becomes a room.

The coffee cup he brings to his eye becomes a telescope.

The room becomes a telephone booth.

Bugs and stars, compass eye, transit of Venus across the sun.

The telephone booth becomes a coffin.

Coffee pot as space ship, journey to the moon.

The coffin becomes a stick figure.

Balance a chair on a finger and the chair will take flight.

The stick figure breaks free and marks the space with lines.

Papers float skyward, backward, the undoing is the doing.

A line flies out of one world and into another, threading them
together.

There's a coffeepot in the eye of the moon.

The figure breaks free and sketches a bone arbor.

A line of people, wounded, crosses the field.

She draws a line in the dirt with her shoe,

They walk into the drawn battlefield of lines.

A quavering trace in an oscillating space. They hold on.

[to ward off the sensor]
[to track the reader][hold on]

—-—

For Marey, the body was an animate machine with invisible workings, and his primary scientific goal was to make those mechanics visible. In the two short pages he devoted to practical applications in his book *Movement*, he wrote "The officers of our army have taken an interest in these researches, and have furnished us with the means of repeating them on a considerable number of soldiers." Marey and assistant Demeny diligently calculated efficiencies, such as the optimum steps per minute to save energy or time. They suggested that soldiers march with bent knees, slightly pitched forward, to conserve energy. They advised when it would be best to transition from a walk to a run. But such practical applications were ultimately peripheral to Marey's quest for scientific understanding. The bird, captured, becomes an evil wizard with a poisonous potion.

American inventor George Eastman patented his paper "stripping film" in 1884 and Marey got his hands on some in 1888. The paper film made chronophotography much more manageable; as a result Marey produced some of the first "motion pictures." One film showed a falling cat twisting in the air and landing on its feet—a phenomenon which seemingly defied the law of angular momentum in physics. But Marey wasn't interested in using the technology to record what we could easily see in life, no matter how entertaining. He wanted to slow the frames down so he could reveal what couldn't be seen otherwise. Because of his resistance to application, Marey's place in the history of cinema has been up for debate. His ambivalence toward film's recreational usage ultimately ended his working relationship with Demeny. The bird, captured, becomes a man who becomes an avenging monster.

Others were not nearly as reluctant to find practical applications for Marey's discoveries. In *Movement*, Marey briefly mentioned how chronophotographs could "show how the stroke of a skilful blacksmith differed from that of a novice." Following this suggestion in 1914, Frank and Lillian Gilbreth, the American founders of "scientific management," adopted Marey's chronophotographic devices in order to improve worker efficiencies and to maximize profits. While their colleague Frederick Winslow Taylor tried to optimize labor with a stopwatch, the Gilbreths used photography and film to capture energy-efficient movements at work and in the home. They claimed that human activity could be divided into seventeen essential motions, and documented the most efficient movements for completing a variety of tasks in their time-motion studies. Their goal was to eliminate wasted motion through standardization. Efficiency ruled the day. The bird, captured, becomes a chimp leader of the ape rebellion.

Future Supreme Court justice Louis Brandeis claimed scientific management strategies would bolster industrial profits, and therefore improve the lives of workers. Lillian Gilbreth claimed that efficient labor practices would "maximize happiness minutes." But these promises were not borne out in reality. The breakdown of labor into component parts, the treatment of the body as a machine, resulted in the breakdown of the human worker. The bird, captured, becomes a hideous goblin with a repulsive voice.

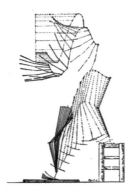

Jump from a height, Marey, *Movement*

How far can the human body be pushed before collapse? Thanks to the science of work, every movement can be evaluated for effort expended, every moment of fatigue registered and recorded. Steps counted, time spent, words spoken. There's a body on the assembly line, reduced to the peaks and valleys of an efficiency chart. The bird, captured, becomes a perpetually drunk captain, a companion in adventure.

They run with the ground shifting beneath their feet. A vine grasps at her ankles, a crack in the earth threatens to swallow him up. Solid land is hard to come by; the wild refuses to cohere as a clear picture. And yet everything quiet, everything still. Just a sliding from one lens to the other.

PART III: FILM STILL

This kind of book is an optical toy where the thumb determines the pace of the pages and the reader has total control. Someone studies the digital exhaust and tilts the worldline in the corner of each page: a gymnast in white shirt and black pants does flips. A slow turbulence of data, a pattern of traces at the end of each paragraph, sets off the actions to come.

"At this moment when flight preoccupies so many researchers, there's the need to understand the behavior of air." So wrote Marey, explaining the logic behind his aerodynamics experiments at the start of the 20th century. Now it's the bird as detective, framed for a future crime.

One of the many researchers preoccupied with mechanized flight was the American astronomer and astrophysicist Samuel Pierpont Langley, who in 1887 was appointed secretary of the Smithsonian Institution. Langley took full advantage of the resources available to him in order to build a viable aircraft. To study the flight of birds, he arranged to buy one of Marey's photographic guns. The two men met at the Universal Exposition in Paris; the following year, Marey wrote to Langley, inquiring if there were any funds available for continuing his research through the Smithsonian, as his Station physiologique was experiencing some budgetary difficulties. Langley encouraged Marey to apply for grant monies that had been left to the Smithsonian specifically for "the investigation of the properties of atmospheric air." Thus, from 1900-1902, Marey's experiments with air in France were funded by an American museum. The bird scrubs the image, looking for clues as to where the murder's going to happen: driver's licenses, the address label on a newspaper, the vectors from shadows.

There's a tall tree ahead that appears stable in both versions of the world—the lush and the barren—so they move toward it carefully.

With each sliding cycle, the differences become more extreme.

Now the vineyards burst with purple grapes on sunny slopes, a god appears in robes of royal purple. Then a non-landscape, a meteor impact site, the scabby earth. Now the wine flows, the nymphs play with tigers and leopards. Then the parched soil, a seam of ore, the fossilized bodies post-carnage. Now a sea of sprouted vines grab and grow as if their legs were arbors. Then the scrubby trees brush, the scorched grass burns, the barbed-wire fences scrape. Now the blood-red wine, the roaring tigers, flutes and tambourines. Then the stony grassland, the strewn viscera, the cyanide-crusted turf. Now a golden throne, a ball of thread. Then a sinkhole, an abandoned mine.

From the height of the tree they think they see a fault line in the distance, the point where the flux of the two worlds stabilizes.

——•——

With the Smithsonian funds, Marey improved upon his last instrument: a smoke machine. An electric fan at the base of the box drew the smoke down in thin streams ("like the strings of a piano") against a black velvet background. The apparatus allowed Marey to track and record the path of air as it flowed around static objects. Though the objects he used were small (capsule shapes, blades of mica, etc.), they were analogies for the wing shapes of airplanes. A federal investigator has come to observe operations. He offers the bird a stick of gum.

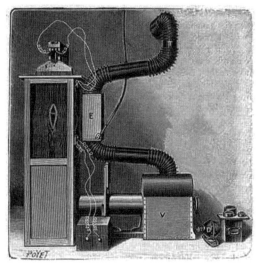

"Les mouvements de l'air étudiés par la chronophotographie,"
Marey, *La Nature*, Sept. 7, 1901

As the smoke trails made contact with the various shapes, they would change course. They wandered, they eddied. Different shapes caused different amounts of drag, made evident by a confusion of smoke, signaling degree of resistance. The shape of the wing defined its conversation with the air. When the confrontation between air and object was lit by the explosion of a magnesium flash, an instant photograph would capture the smoke trails in the acts of deflection and flow. The bird brags to the observer from Justice: Once the Amendment passes, we go national, there's gonna be nowhere to run.

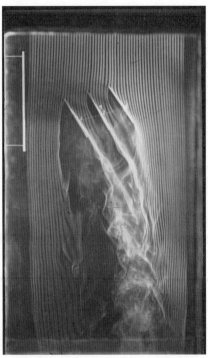

Movements of air around objects, Marey, Collège de France archive

The photographs were modern extensions of the charts and graphic outputs of Marey's earlier instruments and experiments; the white lines on black backgrounds were a kind of memoir written by the air itself. The photographs are legible, readable as text, ready for analysis. Although Marey called these images chronophotographs, they were stills rather than sequences. However, they captured a continuity flowing around a stasis, and in that way they mapped time. The resulting images were instructions for future aviators about the behavior of air currents. Most of our scrambles are flash events like this one, the bird explains to the observer from Justice. We rarely see anything with premeditation anymore.

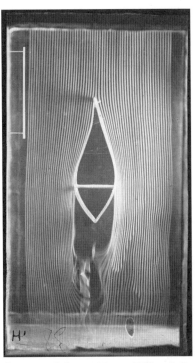

Movements of air around objects, Marey, Collège de France archive

The Smithsonian funding for these experiments was cut off after Langley's research resulted in an ill-advised and failed flight. A year later, in 1903 (a year before Marey's death), the Wright brothers finally succeeded where so many had failed. The brothers had studied Marey's *Animal Mechanism* and *Le Vol de Oiseaux* years before. Marey's ideas and instruments had helped them to connect the dots. The bird's boss is on the line and warns that this is no time for a mistake, the nation votes this week. Don't worry, says the bird.

From the height of the tree they see the radial lines and patterns of outcrop flipping over like waves. In the distance, the fault line is a slender joint of static ground inside the tumult. There is something teeming, a mass migration, on this long seam of earth. At regular intervals, there is an obstacle—a mountain? A rock? The road splits and the swarm divides around the obstruction and reunites on the other side. It's a beautiful pattern with a deadly tail; the end of the seam follows them, transforming land into a cliff abyss. Bodies fall off into the instability.

They do not want to join the swarm. They came all this distance in order to escape the horde. Plus the gamble of the cliff abyss. But their current position isn't viable. With each transformation of the environment, the tree gets older. Its leaves are falling. Small branches are breaking off. It is hollowing out. The surrounding ground in transition is getting wilder and wilder. They run for the middle of the fault line swarm. Or rather, they stutter-run in a stop and start of balance then sprint. They reach the seam.

It is a silent, parched migration. Many wear the wristwatch device. Many have invisible partners. They numbly realize that they were never invisible, never forgotten, had never struck gold. They are statistics in a sizable population, available as any for abuse. They had been sold a bill of goods in their hope for a better life. They had been sold the possibility of freedom from their digital dossiers and restrictive boxing. In fact, they were just two data points on a long sucker list, part of a teaming horde of suckers on a list called "incoherent narratives."

—·—

Marey's smoke machine tracked bodies of air as they moved in response to a disturbance. Charting flows, the data his photographs revealed proved useful to aviators. Photography of the air soon leapt to photography in the air. Wilbur Wright took the first aerial photograph in 1909. During World War I, the aerial photo replaced the battle sketch, the camera positioned in a hole in the floor of the plane. Photographs recorded the field for analysis: trenches, wire entanglements, listening posts, shelters, telephone lines, artillery, anti-tank obstacles causing deflection, disrupting flow. The bird analyzes the data: there's only sixteen of those old merry-go-rounds left in the city—it's gotta be Barnaby Woods.

With aerial photography, soldiers could find streams to cross, trails in the woods, the areas of gumbo ground. Enemy footprints were mapped: searchlights, mobile airdomes, landing tracks. The withering aerial strafe technique in cover of darkness; photoflying required staying above the barrage. A bomb went off and bodies moved in response. Flash bombs for illumination. Infrared to cut through the haze. All the negatives and prints delivered to the photographic interpretation unit for processing. Imagery intelligence. The bird's second-in-command is anxious; Chief, we're catching up to the future.

In peacetime, aerial technique was adapted to map the world: in 1921, Sherman Fairchild mapped New York City; in 1924, the Hamilton Rice Expedition mapped the Amazon. The images were used to understand the land, to chart silting and soil erosion, to take forest inventories, to study the ecology of marshes, the mosaic of crops. Geologists used aerial photos to study the peneplains, the pediments, the steep slopes and flat valleys, the faults and rocky peaks. The bird gets to the scene just in time and makes an arrest, filming everything with grids and vectors.

"Where are we going?" she asks someone in front of her. She hears the echo of several others asking the same question behind her. "The only way we can go" someone answers, a number of people answer. As they walk forward, away from the slowly collapsing end of the seam, they come upon giant stone capsules and cliffs of mica; they flow around them, change course, and reunite further up. Their bodies move in response to the disturbance. To either side, the terrain churns in transformation. She thinks she sees a woman up ahead throw herself into the flux and disappear. But nobody else seems to notice.

A faint buzz, then loud chirping. Above them, two hummingbirds slam into each other.

[sensors][trackers][readers][birds]

—·—

In Hito Steyerl's video *How Not to Be Seen: A Fucking Didactic Educational MOV. File*, a disembodied computer voice instructs the viewer on how to become invisible in plain sight. The set for most of the action is a 1950s resolution target in the California desert. As the video tells us, resolution targets were used by the Air Force in order to calibrate photographs taken from the air. The targets are super-sized Ronchi rulings, groupings of three white bars on black pavement, with each set a different size. They look like eye charts for the sky. As the airplane flies over, the bars articulate the limits of a camera lens' resolution. Because the targets aren't useful for digital imaging, they have become abandoned monuments to old technology. The pavements are cracked, drawing anarchic maps up and through the obedient bar patterns; wild grass bursts through the seams. Whereas the resolution targets were once used to make things visible, they now no longer function. They exist seemingly without purpose. "I wasn't going to do it! I wasn't going to hurt her!" protests the prisoner. But the bird is all business.

Marey spent his life's work trying to make the invisible visible ("seeing the invisible…quite seduces me"); it's a beautifully simple mission. Steyerl's mock-instructional video updates and complicates that goal within a 21st century context. The computer voice declares "Most important things want to remain invisible. Love is invisible. War is invisible. Capital is invisible." For those with privilege, a desired low-profile resolution can be purchased and guaranteed, thanks to gated communities, anti-facial recognition makeup and clothing, or being able to pay someone to scrub your digital presence. For those without such privilege—the disappeared, the poor, the targets of drone strikes—low resolution is a kind of curse. And then there are the undocumented, the exploited laborers who invisibly work behind national scenes, trying to keep their resolution as low as possible so as not to be a caught in the net of deportation. The video instructs "To become invisible one has to become smaller or equal to one pixel." In other words, one has to become (or be perceived as) a disembodied and unvoiced phenomenon: thin air. You ever get any false positives? the observer from Justice asks. The bird is annoyed by the question.

In this procession
they are bits of torn paper

cut-outs in shadow
seen from above
as ribbons of smoke

this helicopter intelligence
these recording birds
of digital revolution

catalog the exhausted paper limbs
the line of bent paper backs
writing the seam

[flip book][to move the reader]
[motion study]

In 1902, two years before his death from liver cancer and too ill to do his own experiments, Marey is reported to have said, "Now I want to watch the others work." But there are different ways to watch others: an observer can be visible or invisible, a spectator or a spy, a bystander or a voyeur. The caretaker explains to the observer from Justice that through optical tomography of the brain, white light pinpoints can be read; we can see what the writhing detectives see.

Would Marey have been interested in the robotic hummingbird, a nano-sized drone, lightweight and equipped with a video camera? Quiet and maneuverable, it can fly in any direction with its two translucent wings. The soldier, pinned down in the valley, pulls it out of his backpack and lets it flap and fly from his palm, and over the ridge. It can perch on a windowsill or a power line and watch, communicating back what it sees. Early in his career Marey had made a series of mechanical birds—ornihopters—that attempted to replicate the motion of flight. He wrote in *Animal Mechanism*, "We hope that we have proved to the reader that nothing is impossible in the analysis of the movements connected with the flight of the bird: he will no doubt be willing to allow that mechanism can always reproduce a movement, the nature of which has been clearly defined." It helps if you don't think of them as human, says the bird to the observer from Justice. They're pattern recognition filters, nothing more.

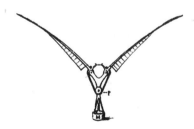

Mechanical bird, Marey, *Vol de Oiseaux*

The nature of the hummingbird spy has been defined as number one in swarm intelligence. There are dangers: wind gusts in the urban canyons, trees that create a wall effect. Its wings produce a steady flow field, a small whirlwind with stable vortices. The bird controls its pitch, roll, and yaw. It hovers with precision. But the bird itself is controlled by a microprocessor connected to a triaxial gyroscope and accelerometer. Blade pitching kinematics power the force. The observer from Justice admits that he's looking for human flaws in the system.

The nano-hummingbird has good company in the air: Silvertone Flamingo, PrecisionHawk Lancaster, EuroHawk, DRDO Imperial Eagle, Golden Hawk, IAI Heron, IAI Bird-Eye, MicroFalcon, Innocon MiniFalcon, EMIT Sparrow, Urban Aeronautics X-Hawk, Border Eagle, Hawk MK V, Raptor, Knight Falcon, NGOs Aviks Lark, Yak Voron Raven, Parrot AR.Drone, FR SWAN X1 Soft Wing, UAS Europe Spy Owl, T-eagle Eye, AeroVironment Raven, Barnes Wallis Swallow, Barnes Wallis Wild Goose, Beechcraft Cardinal, Bell Eagle Eye, Boeing Condor, Boeing ScanEagle, Boeing SolarEagle, DARPA Vulture, Fairchild Bull Goose, General Atomics Grey Eagle, Globe Quail, Honeywell T-Hawk, Lockheed Martin Desert Hawk, Lockheed Martin Cormorant, McDonnell Quail, MMIST Snowgoose, MTC Spy-Hawk, North American Redhead-Roadrunner, Northrop Grumman Global Hawk, Northrop Grumman Firebird, Radioplane Quail, Sea Robin XFC, Vanguard ShadowHawk, XGAM-71 Buck Duck. One of them grabs the bird's finger, holds on to its shirt, speaks to it, clings to it, then finally lets go.

———

As they march, they observe the natural world around them. The stone capsules and cliffs of mica are proliferating and changing. Their smooth surfaces bloom with nubby biometric shrubs. As they march with the migrating swarm, new shapes rise up and force them apart. He signals for her not to touch them, as they are collectors and recorders of accidental contact. Some of the shrubs are covered in beautiful flowers that click with shutters and shots. Someone just ahead of her brushes against a smooth side of mica and it slices a specimen of skin like glass. A stone formation releases radio waves over each body that passes, reflecting its energy back as a three dimensional image in the cloudless sky. The environment reads, tests, and measures.

They notice that their pace is slowing as they climb a steep slope. There's a bottleneck up ahead, as the swarm moves toward a checkpoint with a phalanx of scanners. On the other side of the scanners, a number of cargo planes on the tarmac. They rub their eyes, not quite able to take in what they're seeing in the mirage of the flat sun. A woman with a wristwatch is waved through a scanner and disappears. The guard who waved her through bends down and picks up a book. He flips through it. The book is put in a box. Stacks of boxes are being loaded onto a plane.

—·—

The rhythms of the blood, the patterns of muscular contractions, the geometry of a run, the mechanics of a bird's wing in air: Marey invented the instruments that could turn such movements into a chart of tangible data. Today an algorithm captures our moves from a confusion of smoke: we are the stone capsule, the blade of mica. The algorithm shapes the data into a narrative, a patterned portrait, a packaged profile. Without direct access to our interior, it hypothesizes from the outside in, using a digital sort of 1500 aggregated items into neatly stacked lists:

Platinum Prosperity

Aspirational Fusions—Dare to Dream

Families in Motion—Diapers and Debit Cards

Red, White and Bluegrass

Modest Metro Means

Urban Survivors

Small Town Shallow Pockets

Experian, Acxiom, Datalogix, PeekYou, Rapleaf, Recorded Future: thousands of databrokers sift through the smoke. The bird is beginning to suspect something fishy; it visits the department of containment to take a look at the aggregated datastream.

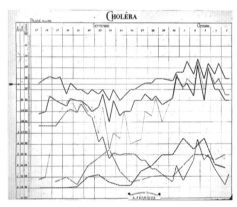

Courbes graphiques multiples du choléra, Marey, Collège de France

Marey was an early dataminer. In 1884, he interrupted his experiments with chronophotography in order to help track the source of a cholera outbreak in Paris. From his hometown of Beaune, he sat down with doctors' records of fatalities and laid them on top of maps of Parisian waterways—the streams and canals and sewers. The cartographic layering revealed a singular pattern of coincidence that made the source of the problem (fecal contamination of water) apparent. The sentry warns the bird: Careful Chief…You dig up the past, all you get is dirty.

Each move we make creates a line drawn, a filament of smoke: addresses, driving records, voter registration, credit card purchases, bank card transactions, health care records, web browsing histories, social media posts. The aspiration for the datamined profile is a mirror image of the subject through smoke: to pass the test, to be a real human. The reality is more likely an error-prone doppelganger, made of bits and pieces. You'll never meet your data-double (it is proprietary), but it will follow you for all of your life. Corporations will flirt with your double and buy it dinner in the hopes of getting to know you and what you might buy, what you might watch, whom you might vote for, what health procedures or prescriptions you might pursue. They will seduce your double so as to determine a price, deny you a loan or a service, limit your job opportunities, or give you a longer jail sentence. Your double eagerly tells wacky half-truths about you to whomever will buy it a drink. It is a blabber-mouth. The bird reports his findings to his boss, who says Remember, the eyes of the nation are on us right now. The bird looks the old man in the eye.

Ultimately, Marey was a reader. His method was to hunt and capture the imperceptible and make it legible. He wanted to turn movement into writing—the long swirls of script moving out one window and into the next—but not into narrative: the pages before they've been thumbed into motion. He didn't care about commercial applications, or what his inventions made possible. He was simply a mechanic who made instruments to measure the physiological machine. While scrubbing the image and sorting through the data, suddenly the bird's own face is revealed as the killer.

A tool can be used for science or commerce, for inquiry or profit. Marey lived in a time and a place where the two could be comfortably separated. It's starting to sink in for the bird that its life has changed forever, that it's now and forever a hunted bird. The bird swaps out its eyes to evade the scanners.

—·—

When they see the books, the cargo, they must make a choice. They shuffle to the perimeter of the bottleneck, to the very edge of the pavement. To either side of the road, the earth continues to roil in violent whirlpools drawing the debris of the world down into their deep eyes. Every so often the whirlpools transform into flat calm seas or idyllic green pastures, only to collapse like crumpled paper thrown into a bottomless vortex.

The road continues to convey forward, with its deadly drop-off tail at the back. They begin to understand that the bottleneck is not so much due to congestion, as it is to hesitation and then a small group of resisters. They decide to join the scanner resistance, while most don't recognize the choice and plod forward toward the inexorable. The resistance strategy is simple: slow down. There's a thin red thread unraveling from hand to hand—if they hold onto it, they can hold themselves back. They do this, knowing that eventually the end of the road will catch up with them.

This is the first time they've talked since the device was implanted in her wrist. The red thread makes them think of Ariadne's thread, how it showed the way out of the labyrinth.

They talk about how Dionysus took Ariadne from Theseus, and when she died, he put her image in the sky.

They talk about how seeing constellations requires connecting the points with an invisible narrative thread.

POPULAR SCIENCE

"Precise experiment and exact measurement," wrote Marey, "have begun to appear even in the phenomena of thought." I discuss this chronometric experimentation to show that the science of data collection was beginning to affect the cerebral. The darkness shrank before science.

    —Francois Dagognet, *Étienne-Jules Marey: A Passion
      for the Trace*

…instead of revealing the beautiful complexity at our core, we live in a culture where dull biological platitudes make headlines and irritating scientific clichés win arguments. In response, we do not need a simpler culture but one that embraces complexity.

    —Vaughan Bell, "Our Brains and How They're Not As Simple
      as We Think"

If you look at the PET scan, I look just like one of those killers

    —James Fallon on "Morning Edition," NPR

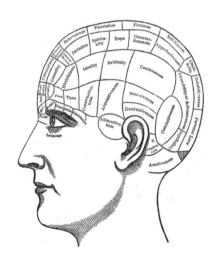

Not long ago, about the closing in of an evening in autumn, I searched and scrolled near the large bay window of D— Coffee-House in Philadelphia and happened upon an interesting literary footnote: In 1849, six years prior to the first edition of *Leaves of Grass*, Walt Whitman visited the Phrenological Cabinet of Fowler & Wells to get his head examined.

the pulses of your brain await their chance

Phrenology—the science of discerning one's character by mapping and measuring the shape of the skull—first appeared in 1796, with the research of a German neuroanatomist named Franz Joseph Gall, who went on to publish a book called *The Anatomy and Physiology of the Nervous System in General, and of the Brain in Particular, with Observations upon the possibility of ascertaining the several intellectual and moral dispositions of man and animal by the configuration of their Heads.*

According to Gall's system, each hill and groove on the surface of the skull represents the location of specific mental faculties beneath; a person could be known simply through intent observation and gentle prodding of the cranium. In 1832 Gall's collaborator, J.G. Spurzheim, introduced phrenology to the United States, where it was popularized by brothers Lorenzo and Orson Fowler, who were later joined by an associate, Samuel Roberts Wells. With offices in Philadelphia, New York, and Boston, and a publishing arm that produced books, pamphlets, self-help manuals, and journals, Fowler & Wells made phrenology a national sensation. In addition to Whitman, those who presented their skulls for analysis included Margaret Fuller, Oliver Wendell Holmes, Allan Pinkerton, Mark Twain, and Horace Mann.

After poring over advertisements for indispensable handbooks and illustrated "cyclopedias," I peered through the smoky glass into the street. It was getting dark and rush hour was in full swing. I wasn't sure, but I thought I caught a glimpse of a familiar figure in the sidewalk throng, then lost sight of him. I turned back to my work.

they seep between regions
cover the entire surface
a faint blue veneer

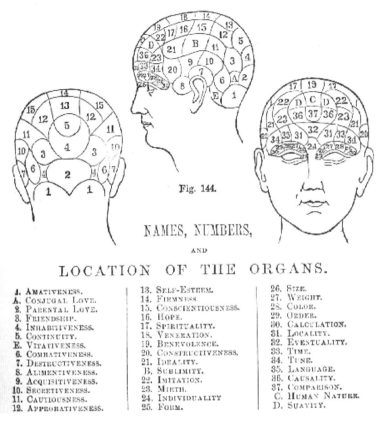

Fig. 144.

NAMES, NUMBERS,

AND

LOCATION OF THE ORGANS.

1. AMATIVENESS.
A. CONJUGAL LOVE.
2. PARENTAL LOVE.
3. FRIENDSHIP.
4. INHABITIVENESS.
5. CONTINUITY.
E. VITATIVENESS.
6. COMBATIVENESS.
7. DESTRUCTIVENESS.
8. ALIMENTIVENESS.
9. ACQUISITIVENESS.
10. SECRETIVENESS.
11. CAUTIOUSNESS.
12. APPROBATIVENESS.

13. SELF-ESTEEM.
14. FIRMNESS.
15. CONSCIENTIOUSNESS.
16. HOPE.
17. SPIRITUALITY.
18. VENERATION.
19. BENEVOLENCE.
20. CONSTRUCTIVENESS.
21. IDEALITY.
B. SUBLIMITY.
22. IMITATION.
23. MIRTH.
24. INDIVIDUALITY
25. FORM.

26. SIZE.
27. WEIGHT.
28. COLOR.
29. ORDER.
30. CALCULATION.
31. LOCALITY.
32. EVENTUALITY.
33. TIME.
34. TUNE.
35. LANGUAGE.
36. CAUSALITY.
37. COMPARISON.
C. HUMAN NATURE.
D. SUAVITY.

Whitman submitted his skull for review by the Fowlers more than once (the first report concluded that Whitman "by practice might make a good accountant"). He reprinted his favorite phrenological summary five times—once in an anonymous review of his own work. The tenets of phrenology happily confirmed his self-concept:

Leading traits of character appear to be Friendship, Sympathy, Sublimity, and Self-Esteem, and markedly among his combinations the dangerous faults of Indolence, a tendency to the pleasures of Voluptuousness and Alimentiveness, and a certain reckless swing of animal will, too unmindful, probably, of the conviction of others.

"[You] did not get ripe like a hothouse plant but you can last long and grow better": from Walt Whitman's first phrenological report, written by Lorenzo Fowler, 1849.

Although Whitman's love affair with phrenology eventually came to an end as the practice fell out of favor, I found traces of it scattered throughout the drafts and final versions of his poems. "Song of the Broadaxe" (which first appeared in the second edition of *Leaves of Grass*, published by Fowler & Wells in 1856) celebrates the individualized "shapes of America" as well as the faculties listed in Whitman's phrenological chart:

> Never offering others, always offering himself, corroborating his
>   phrenology,
> Voluptuous, inhabitive, combative, conscientious, alimentive,
>   intuitive, of copious friendship, sublimity, firmness, self-
>   esteem, comparison, individuality, form, locality, eventuality,
> Avowing by life, manners, works, to contribute illustrations of
>   results of The States...

The poems "Faces," "Mediums," and "By Blue Ontario's Shore" also make use of phrenology's terms.

> "My brain, it shall be your occult convolutions"
> "To feed the greed of the belly the brain is liberally spooning"
> "All beauty comes from beautiful blood and a beautiful brain"
> "The pulses of your brain waiting their chance"

Eventually I left D— Coffee-House and joined the waver, jostle and hum. Navigating the narrow city sidewalks, we moved in co-ordinated relation, a sea of human heads. Although I knew not my fellow passengers, I recognized their types: businessmen, administrative assistants, med students, working mothers, etc. And then, up ahead—could it be?—the familiar figure. I pushed through the crowd in his direction, but he had already disappeared.

the pulses swarm, flock, shoal

Weeks later, passing time at an airport newsstand, I noticed several magazines with cover stories on the brain: *Time* had a cartoonish image riffing on Spurzheim's diagram with a headline announcing the "Science of Optimism: Hope isn't rational—so why are humans wired for it?" *Scientific American Mind* featured a story about the "weird" brains of creative people. *Psychology Today*'s main story, "Clues to Character," listed a set of "stable traits" that help predict behavior; knowing these traits could help you find a partner or evaluate a job candidate. The soft science of Whitman's day—with its desire to attach character traits to specific regions of the brain—seemed alive and well in the popular press.

In organized formation, several planes arrived in close succession. Suddenly the corridor filled with a swarm of bodies heading toward baggage claim, each looking for the gap that would allow progress forward. I recognized the looks, the tired faces energized by the release onto solid ground. I recognized the purposeful pace and pattern.

The nineteenth-century doctrine of the skull eventually gave way to the twentieth-century doctrine of the neuron, and the sideshow spectacle of phrenology was deemed a pseudo-science. By the twenty-first century, functional magnetic resonance imaging as well as positron emission tomography, electroencephalography, and computerized axial tomography were busy gathering concrete proof of various locational neuronal theories. At least that's the way it seemed, as I read about the areas of the brain lighting up while waiting in the gate area.

We boarded, in an order, a coalition of partners. The plane was packed and we began the negotiation of how to sit so close together and yet maintain our personal space. As we sat facing forward, the plane followed the dotted line of a predetermined trajectory from here to there. First this, then that. When we arrived, we filed off the plane and were released onto solid ground. We were free of each other but continued to move in relation, a system of interacting dynamics.

as crickets sync
they merge and sing in a changing cycle
femurs against forewings

Back at home, a thick humid fog hung over the city, and the streets seemed empty. In the library this time, I continued my research. Could the brain fit inside a single sentence? I turned the pages, hoping for the film from the mental vision to depart, peering through the smoky panes into the street. Thirty-seven mental and moral faculties. Eighty billion neurons with trillions of synaptic connections between them. Centers or systems? Symmetry-making or symmetry-breaking? I was hitting up against a language problem. I looked at the words in their aggregate relations. Until very late at night.

"Leading traits of character appear to be Friendship, Sympathy, Sublimity, and Self-Esteem…"

Illustration 1: Friendship
(also called ADHESIVENESS)

3. ADHESIVENESS.

Situated on each side of Concentrativeness, higher up than Philoprogenitiveness, just above the lambdoidal suture. The medial prefrontal cortex signals someone of value. Frontal systems linked with limbic circuits facilitate love of friends. Coping with frenemies. Judgments about the close others inoroasod blood oxygenation level-dependent response along the frontal midline. I have seen boys, also, walk in the street with their arms twined around each other's necks, and always in each other's society. They say they love each other very much. Social closeness is the primary factor, rather than shared beliefs, as previously assumed. It is right, children, to exercise this organ. Regions that respond to information about friends are shown in orange; regions that respond more to strangers are in blue. While in the scanner they played "The Newlywed Game": would a friend or stranger prefer an aisle or window seat? Sheep skip and play together in the open field. This is true of almost all animals, and they, with us, have a little prominence on their skulls, caused by the development of the brain, which we call Adhesiveness. Sure enough, the bigger the amygdala, the larger and more complex a person's

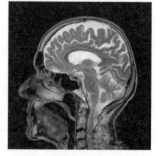

social network tended to be. Mlle. N. "was so tenderly attached to a lady of her own age, that neither marriage nor the solicitations of her mother could induce her to leave her." This finding is exciting because it opens a window into exploring abnormalities in the amygdala. The

organ is large in Mrs. H. and Mary Macinnes—Established. For more on how experience changes the brain, check out my new book.

George Combe, *Elements of Phrenology*; "Brain responds more to close friends, imaging study shows," *Science Daily*; Krienen, Tu, and Buckner, "Clan Mentality: Evidence that Medial Prefrontal Cortex Responds to Close Others," *Journal of Neuroscience*; Kirsten Weir, "Fickle Friends: How to Deal with Frenemies," *Scientific American Mind*; Lydia Folger Fowler, *Familiar Lessons on Phrenology: Designed for the Use of Children and Youth*; Susan Weinschenk, "100 Things You Should Know About People: #88—Your Brain Has A Special Response to People You Know," *The Team W Blog*; Jeanna Bryner, "Brains Hard-Wired to Connect with Friends," *LiveScience.com*; Sian Beilock, "When It Comes to Our Social Networks, Brain Size Matters," *Psychology Today*; Samuel Roberts Wells, *How to Read Character: A New Illustrated Hand-book of Phrenology*.

forming and re-forming

In 1849 (the same year as Whitman's first phrenological exam), in an article published in the *American Phrenological Journal*, the Fowler brothers wrote "Our present desire is this—TO PHRENOLO-GIZE OUR NATION, for thereby it will REFORM THE WORLD." 1849 was also the year when the United States Department of the Interior was established. Manifest destiny was in full force.

LARGE.   SMALL.

FIG. 118.—ARTEMUS WARD.*   FIG. 119.—KANOSH, AN INDIAN CHIEF.

According to Samuel Wells in *How to Read Character*, "the organ of Mirthfulness is situated on the side of the upper part of the forehead." The illustration above was presented as proof, with a footnote stating "Mr. Charles F. Brown, better known as 'Artemus Ward,' was one of the most noted of American humorists. Mirthfulness is seen to be very well developed. The contrast between his head and that of the Indian Chief is very striking." In phrenology, bigger was always better. If an organ area was found to be "small," the Fowlers provided tips on how to exercise the region so as to promote its growth. The brain, like the body, was a muscle to be worked. If the Indian Chief wished to enlarge that portion of his brain associated with mirth, he was advised:

The facetious aspects of things and subjects should be contemplated, and the idea that dignity and self-respect require perpetual seriousness must be resolutely combated. The company of mirthful people should be sought, for nothing is more contagious than genuine jollity. There is a time to laugh as well as a time to weep, and laughter is promotive of health and longevity. The injunction to "laugh and grow fat!" is not without a physiological reason, nor is the Shaksperian adage that "a light heart lives long," a mere poetical flourish.

But of course this instruction wasn't meant for the Indian Chief.

aggregate choruses
temporary unisons that then move on

Mark Twain had his skull read several times by Lorenzo Fowler; the first time he used an assumed name, and the phrenological report revealed a cavity that "represented a total absence of the sense of humor." When he returned for a second reading a few months later (this time with a calling card stating his real name as well as his pen name), the cavity suddenly transformed into a lofty bump of mirthfulness. He wrote of his visits to Fowler: "These experiences have given me a prejudice against phrenology which has lasted until now. I am aware that the prejudice should have been against Fowler, instead of against the art   But, I am human, and that is not the way prejudices act."

The frontal lobe is the only part of the brain where a phrenological mapping coincides with a contemporary assignment of functional location: the faculty of "mirthfulness" is said to be exactly where the left prefrontal cortex lights up on fMRI scans when people are happy.

a glacier of fluids,
the coincidence of their calls

Illustration 2: Sympathy (also called BENEVOLENCE)

19. BENEVOLENCE.

Directly in front of Veneration is a piece of brain that induces us to be kind hearted. Some people lack those feelings and may behave in anti-social ways that can be extremely costly to society. Oxytocin is known as the "love hormone" because it encourages trust, cooperation and social bonding. Suppressed when the story content and expression were mismatched; having a person smile while telling about his mother's death. You can restrain excesses, and can cultivate deficiencies. You may be intellectual, you may be social, but the moral nature is the "crown of glory," and nothing can atone for the absence of it, or supply its place. Activation in the ventromedial prefrontal cortex and superior frontal gyrus, regions that deal with social conflict. Men have more of this working Benevolence than women, and it is proper they should have, as their power to help is greater; but women are more sympathetic and more readily touched by pity. Murderers generally have the forehead "villainously low" in the region of Benevolence. People with low activity in the orbital cortex are either free-wheeling types or sociopaths. When Destructiveness is large and this organ small, cruelty may result. Dutch men who inhaled oxytocin were more likely to associate positive words, such as joy and laughter, and complex positive emotions, such as hope and admiration, with Dutch people than with Germans or Arabs. It has been objected that Nature cannot

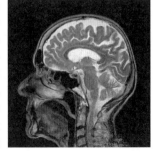

have placed a faculty of Benevolence, and another of Destructiveness, in the same mind; but Man is confessedly an assemblage of contradictions. All can improve if they have the desire; restrain your feelings and that organ will increase in size; the brain will enlarge, and

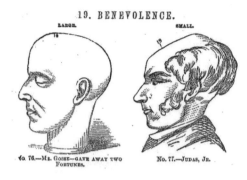

19. BENEVOLENCE.

No. 76.—Mr. Gosse—Gave away two fortunes.

No. 77.—Judas, Jr.

will press out the skull. A very basic way we connect to other people.

Lydia Folger Fowler, *Familiar Lessons on Phrenology: Designed for the Use of Children and Youth*; "Search for Sympathy Uncovers Patterns of Brain Activity," *Science Daily*; Janelle Weaver, "The Prejudice Hormone: Oxytocin, Known for Encouraging Bonding, May Underlie Bias," *Scientific American Mind*; Clara Moskowitz, "Neuroscience May Explain the Dalai Lama," *NBCNews.com*; Samuel Roberts Wells, *How to Read Character: A New Illustrated Hand-book of Phrenology*; Barbara Bradley Hagerty, "A Neuroscientist Uncovers A Dark Secret," *NPR*; George Combe, *Elements of Phrenology*.

the pulses of the brain await their chance

According to the tenets of phrenology, interior traits are legible, an open territory to be read and analyzed. The head is a map of self-help; all flaws can be conquered, rewritten, perfected. As Walt Whitman wrote in response to first hearing a lecture by Orson Fowler, "If the professor can, as he professes, teach men to know their intellectual and moral deficiencies and remedy them, we do not see that our people may long remain imperfect."

"Our people" was a category limited to those with white skin; it was the white person who could benefit from the brain's flexibility and all others were stuck with an array of imperfect presets. Thus, the discourse of phrenology attached itself to a long history of discriminatory nationalisms and racist essentialisms:

> The special organs in which the Caucasian brain most excels, and which distinguish it from those of all less advanced races, are Mirthfulness, Ideality, and Conscientiousness, the organs of these faculties being almost invariably small in savage and barbarous tribes. (Wells, vii)

> The breadth of the wings of the nose next to the face indicates Secretiveness. This is in accordance with the physiological action of this faculty which tends to shut the mouth and expand the nostrils. This sign is large in the Negro, the Chinese, the North American Indian and in most savage and half-civilized tribes. (Wells, 63)

FIG. 16.—BLACK HAWK.   FIG. 17.—JOSEPH SMITH.   FIG. 20.—EMANUEL KANT.   FIG. 21.—A NEGRO.
                    THE SOCIAL GROUP.   REFLECTIVE GROUP.

Today, it is proposed that if the rationalism of the prefrontal cortex could suppress the emotionality produced by the amygdala and the ventral striatum, perhaps racism could be prevented. Newsstand magazines and digital clickbait tell us the prefrontal cortex is our best hope. There was the neuroscientist who had a number of murderers in his family tree. Upon reviewing his own brain scan, he discovered that his orbital cortex—the area of the brain thought to control ethical behavior and impulse control—was inactive. He wondered, might he be a psychopath-in-waiting? For the phrenologists, the link of location to behavior provided a seductive narrative structure of legible cause and effect. If this, then that. In the article about the neuroscientist, I sensed the allure of that structure still simmering.

Illustration 3: SUBLIMITY

Situated on the side-head, directly above Acquisitiveness and behind Ideality, the dough-nut-shaped machine swallows the nun. A high-tech attempt to read her mind as she communes with her deity. The vast, the grand, the majestic: Is there a God spot in the brain? Pin down what happens in the brain when people experience mystical awakenings. One with large Sublimity would enjoy scenery similar to that represented in the cut. When the Buddhists lost their sense of existence as separate individuals, the researchers injected them with a radioactive isotope that is carried by the blood to active brain areas. It is designed to represent the waters rushing and tumbling over the rocks at the Falls of Niagara. A large drop in activity in a portion of the parietal lobe, which encompasses the back of the brain, and an increase in activity in the right prefrontal cortex, which resides behind the forehead. They love the cragged precipice, the snow-capped mountain, the raging cataract, the burning volcano. Because the affected part of the parietal lobe normally aids with navigation and spatial orientation, the neuroscientists surmise that its abnormal silence during medita-

tion underlies the perceived dissolution of physical boundaries and the feeling of being at one with the universe. Some would like to sail on the mighty ocean when the angry waves and billows rise around their tempest-tossed ship. fMRI scans of several hundred Buddhist brains from around the world. Sublimity enables us to appreciate mountain scenery, the

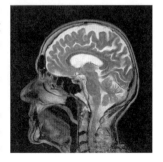

vastness of the ocean, the grandeur of a thunder-storm, the roar of artillery, the clash of armies, etc. It is possible that some people's brains will simply resist succumbing to the divine. Nature deficit disorder.

Samuel Roberts Wells, *How to Read Character: A New Illustrated Hand-book of Phrenology*; David Biello, "Searching for God in the Brain," *Scientific American Mind*; Ian Sample, " 'God spot' researchers see the light in MRI study," *The Guardian*; Matt Danzico, "Brains of Buddhist Monks scanned in Meditation Study," *BBC News*; Lydia Folger Fowler, *Familiar Lessons on Phrenology: Designed for the Use of Children and Youth*.

as bodies of starlings in cloudstorm
form, splay, and re-form

In 1838, Orson Fowler opened a Philadelphia office with his brother-in-law at 210 Chestnut Street. According to Madeleine Stern, in her book *Heads & Headlines: The Phrenological Fowlers*, this "phrenological museum," contained the "rarest assemblage, perhaps, on this continent of unique skulls, and casts of persons now living… nearly, if not wholly, unparalleled in the series of cranioscopal formations." Fowler began to publish *The American Phrenological Journal and Miscellany*, which almost instantly plunged his practice into financial ruin. The office closed in 1842; however a new office and bookstore opened in 1854 (this time in partnership with Samuel Wells) at 231 Arch Street.

I decided to visit the sites of these former offices. The United States Custom House (built during the Depression) occupied the location of Orson Fowler's first office. On what I believed to be the site of the second office was a red brick building, with the name "Berger Brothers Company" just barely visible above the first floor. Berger Brothers was a supplier for tinners and roofers in the 1920s.

After mapping these coordinates, I learned that all of the street numbers in Philadelphia were changed in 1857 and my conclusions regarding the sites of the phrenological offices were entirely misinformed. I had tried to understand historical events through location, driven by the belief that if I could see the architectural skeleton, the ghosts of intrinsic structure, perhaps I could understand what had happened at a moment in time. I had placed my hopes on a stabilized regional genealogy, on the pleasures of equating that with this.

pulled together by the simplest of rules:
don't get too close,
don't get too far from your neighbor

Illustration 4: SELF ESTEEM

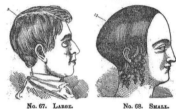

13. SELF-ESTEEM.

No. 67. Large.   No. 68. Small.

Situated at the vertex of the top-head, where the coronal surface begins to decline. She called on God on every occasion, as if he took a special interest in her affairs. The drive system can turn to the system that will give it a proverbial spanking or the system that will give it a hug. We may attack ourselves. Children with this organ large, think they can do as much as their parents; and often feel as though they were too old to render obedience to their requests, running on oxytocin and intrinsic opiates. Some one is always the head, the captain, or the ruling spirit, and all the others do as he dictates. This makes sense to me from the sociometer perspective. The imposter phenomenon. One man always rules, and another serves; one man makes the laws of the nation, and another obeys them. If a person speaks to another at all disrespectfully, the latter feels that he must challenge him to fight a duel, and endeavor to take his life.

Anatomy-based diffusion tensor imaging. Sometimes the organ is too large, and gives a haughty domineering spirit, as is manifested in the cut. She spreads out her beautiful feathers. He saw his violent clients as egotists with a grandiose sense of personal superiority and entitlement. There are persons who are exceedingly censorious, whose conversation is habitually directed to their neighbours'

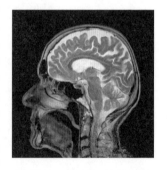

faults, who feel sore when others are elevated, and experience great pleasure in bringing them down. Many schools have students make lists of reasons why they are wonderful people or sing songs of self-celebration. Children in hooting and pelting an idiot. Positively correlated with the degree of self-reported social distress experienced during a game of cyberball. Their chief motive is a strong sense of their own superiority. She held her head high and a little backwards. Your brain maintains complex maps for the "pecking order" of the people surrounding you. Self-Esteem corresponds in some measure to the Desire of Power of the metaphysicians. They could see an avatar. It disposes to the use of the emphatic I in writing and conversation. "I am a man," Black

Fig.10.—Self-Esteem.

Hawk said to Jackson. Changes in pecking order brings about changes in how millions of neurons are connected. When the organ becomes excited by disease, the individual is prone to imagine himself a king, emperor, or a transcendent genius, and some have even fancied themselves the Supreme Being. The organ is large in Haggart, the Hindoos, Dempsey; moderate in Dr. Hette, and the American Indians.— Established. Cross-lagged analysis. With more dopamine and other "happy" neurochemicals, an increase in status increases the number of new connections made per hour in the brain.

Samuel Roberts Wells, *How to Read Character: A New Illustrated Hand-book of Phrenology*; George Combe, *Elements of Phrenology*; Robin Nixon, "The Neuroscience of Self-Esteem, Self-Criticism and Self-Compassion," *LiveScience.com*; Lydia Folger Fowler, *Familiar Lessons on Phrenology: Designed for the Use of Children and Youth*; Roy F. Baumeister, "Violent Pride," *Scientific American Mind*; Keiichi Onoda et. al., "Does low self-esteem enhance social pain?," *Social Cognitive and Affective Neuroscience*; David Rock "Has Coddling an Entire Generation of Children Set Them Up for Failure?," *Psychology Today*.

everyday agents sufficiently stirred
by the earth's rotation

In his essay, "Nature," Emerson wrote, "Parts of speech are metaphors because the whole of nature is a metaphor of the human mind." And as nature changes, so do the metaphors. For instance: Hemispheres. Water systems, dams, plumbing. A city, a village. A lost sailor catches a faint glimpse of a lighthouse. A sailor jumps for joy. Cortex bark. Dendrite trees. A piano with a limited number of keys producing an unlimited number of melodies. A steam engine. A railway switching system. A telegraph relays as neurons. An automated factory. A telephone exchange; behavior like a phone call patched through. A train routed to the right track. An adding machine. A library machine. A mechanical calculator. A part going down the assembly line. Crowding problems, traffic jams. A noisy stadium. Lock and key. Photograph as memory. An enchanted loom "where millions of flashing shuttles weave a dissolving pattern." Hydraulic automatons. Nerves are pipes in the system. Croquet. Oscillators. Marbles. Gyroscopes. A Swiss Army knife. A nerve breathes. Wires. The synapse valve. A piano playing a song expressed in cortical vibrations generating thoughts. Gunpowder burning its way down the axon. Diodes, triodes, multi-vibrators. A synapse as resistor, a rheostat. Hardware. Software. Coupled oscillators. Brain as amplifier. A holograph. A computer. A small world network. Parts light up.

wandering stars, confined to no orbit

Illustration 5: Indolence

No. 53. LARGE.   No. 54. SMALL.

Below and in front of Alimentiveness, we find the region of Relaxation. The premotor cortex tends to light up. The lymphatick, or phlegmatick, levels of dopamine. The machine tracked the flow of oxygenated blood, indicated by soft and abundant flesh, and languor of the pulse. A dull, ease-seeking, inefficient temperament could be more about biology than attitude. If a heated atmosphere had been best for man, Nature would have heated it; but it relaxes. The result is a rollercoaster of hippocampal activity depending on the street network. Unless you would make stupid blockheads of your children, do not keep them shut up in a hot-stove room. Distinctions between brains of the apathetic vs. go-getters. A flattened crown indicates a want of ambition, energy, and aspiration. Navigating with GPS is making our brains lazy. Breathe abundantly so as to turn up the surplus

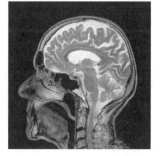

carbon; sit little, but walk much. A treatment for those pathological conditions of extreme apathy.

Joseph Rhodes Buchanan, *Buchanan's Journal of Man*; Robert Roy Britt, "Laziness: Blame it on the Brain?," *LiveScience.com*; Orson Squire Fowler, *Fowler's Practical Phrenology*; Rob Verger, "Navigating with GPS is Making Our Brains Lazy," *Popular Science*; Orson Squire Fowler, *Science of Life: Its Principles, Faculties, Organs, Temperaments*; Orson Squire Fowler, *The Practical Phrenologist*.

a pattern imposed on flow
a swarm of small causes in the tent city of neurons

The language of cure is the language of knowing where you are on the map. A bump on the head, a signal of electrical activity, moving down the line from fault to perfection, a localized equivalency. This is the physical script of the modular mind, the narrative arc of see-then-solve. The dream of clean borders and limited cross-overs. The perpetual re-searching for cause and explanation. The desire for a leader, a general, a man at the top.

In opposition, a familiar figure wanders in convolutions, merging with a crowd just leaving a stadium. He moves in response to all the other moves, changing and shifting in relation. A collaboration of parts leading to some form, wired for reciprocity, a response and in turn a stimulus. In other words, a conversation, changing and shifting in circumstance. Everyone finds their way home.

As patterns of being web forward in integrative networks, the defenders of states' rights and strong borders feel the waters rising. They see the regions shifting, dispersing, and they fight for the static quo. Waiting for a small patch of gray matter to light up the night and diagnose the diseases of the mental landscape in a pinpoint.

protesting at the edges of cities, within private parks,
beside city halls, on campus lawns

Meanwhile, a figure wandering in convolutions responds with flux, resists the spell of the positron emission, the colorful diagram, the photogenic splice. Behavior colors outside the lines, always on the lam, falling off the map—an unruly region, messing up the works, merging with other processes. Not a mass action, but interactive, spatially responsive, ongoing.

I want to be that figure. Instead I seek the pleasures of neat equations and clean comparisons. My premotor cortex lights up. I crave the narrative structure of that equals this. Lazy brain.

Illustration 6: Voluptuousness (also called AMATIVENESS)

PARENTAL LOVE VERY LARGE, AMATIVENESS DEFICIENT.

NO. 209.—THE DEVOTED MOTHER, BUT INDIFFERENT WIFE.

This organ is located at the back of the head, behind the ears and gives fulness to the neck. A computer-generated map of particularly active areas showed hot spots deep in the brain, below conscious awareness, in areas called the caudate nucleus and the ventral tegmental area, which communicate with each other as part of a circuit. To find it, feel on the middle line toward the base of the skull, at the back part of the head, and you will discover a small bony projection called the occipital process. Close your eyes for a minute and envision all the romantic parts of the human body. Another area that lit up produces dopamine, a powerful neurotransmitter that affects pleasure and motivation. Considerable humidity of the lip. Her front brain is telling her he's trouble, but her middle brain won't listen. Aaron Burr, third Vice-President of the United States, was noted for his debauchery in private life, as well as for his unscrupulous conduct as a statesman. Bet you didn't think about the caudate and the ventral tegmental areas, did you? The men had quite a bit more activity in the brain region that

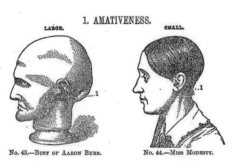

1. AMATIVENESS.

LARGE.   SMALL.

No. 43.—BUST OF AARON BURR.   No. 44.—MISS MODESTY.

integrates visual stimuli. This isn't surprising considering that men support the porn industry and women spend their lives trying to look good for men. Besotted volunteers in a brain scanner. Any one desiring to cultivate Amativeness, then, should go into society as much as

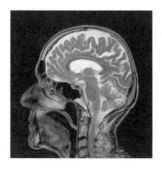

convenient, make it a point to be agreeable as possible to those persons of the other sex. You can almost imagine a time where instead of going to Match.com you could have a test to find out whether you're an attachment type or not. If this organ be perverted, or used improperly, it is the means of making men and women very unhappy, and very wicked. Being dumped actually does heighten romantic love, a phenomenon called frustration-attraction. Little blind boy Cupid with a bow and arrow. M.R.I. images, in the caudate nucleus. Excesses are by no means always referable to the organ in the brain. The true cause is often gastric irritation.

Lydia Folger Fowler, *Familiar Lessons on Phrenology: Designed for the Use of Children and Youth*; Benedict Carey, "Watching New Love as It Sears the Brain," *The New York Times*; Samuel Roberts Wells, *How to Read Character: A New Illustrated Hand-book of Phrenology*; Elizabeth Cohen, "Loving with all your… brain," *CNN*; "Discovering the Mysteries of Love and the Brain," *Los Angeles Times*; Emily Eakin, "Looking for That Brain Wave Called Love: Humanities Experts Use M.R.I.'s to Scan the Mind for the Locus of the Finer Feelings," *The New York Times*.

the pulses travel the same currents

Edgar Allan Poe moved to Philadelphia in the same year Orson Fowler opened his office on Chestnut Street; in fact Poe's publisher worked out of the same building. Although they never met, I imagine Poe and the phrenologists walking the same streets, drinking in the same bars. The result of Poe taking one path while the Fowlers take another creates a circuit in the atmosphere, cells only, pulsing on a matrix of currents.

References to phrenology can be found in a number of Poe's stories (see "Imp of the Perverse," "The Murders in the Rue Morgue," "Ligeia"), but there is no evidence that Poe ever submitted his skull to be analyzed. And though the Fowlers may not have known Poe, they used him (and *not* Walt Whitman) as the embodiment of the "poet's temperament"—nervous and high-strung. After Poe died, the Fowlers released a conjectural phrenological report. His strengths were in the faculties of Ideality, Sublimity, Spirituality, and Language. His weakness was Bibativeness (situated in front of Alimentiveness, near the ears):

> The wine-cup was the bane of his being, and brought out the worst phases of his character; and although his friends claim that this one fault was the procurer of all his waywardness and gained him all his enemies, yet we believe that, artificial excitement aside, he was from the very nature of his organization a wandering star, which could be confined to no orbit and limited to no constellation in the empire of mind.

In my newsfeed I see reports of various stars breaking out of rehab. In *Scientific American Mind*, I find an updated location for bibativeness:

> An alcoholic's problems with social cues are consistent with the "frontal lobe hypothesis," which postulates that damage to the prefrontal cortex—known to be vulnerable to alcohol's toxic effects— leads to behavioral deficits.

constellatory matter repositioning

Illustration 7: ALIMENTIVENESS

8. ALIMENTIVENESS.

Regions of the brain linked with pleasurable emotions and sensations—particularly the nucleus accumbens in the ventral striatum. Nearly parallel with the zygomatic arch, exactly under the organ of Acquisitiveness, and before that of Destructiveness. When the teenager was given normal levels of the hormone, brain imaging showed greater activity in the striatum, an area associated with reward. When the organ is large, the head is broad at this part, resulting in an overlapping of flabby integument, which gives a gross animal look to the face. Some appear to have fewer dopamine D2 receptors in key reward regions of the brain than other people—much like drug addicts. Which must not be confounded with high cheek-bones. One should make his table and its belongings as attractive as possible. These brain scans are of an obese teenager whose fat cells were unable to secrete leptin. In the cut, you will see two men very busy with their knives and forks, etc. Thus, it is pos-

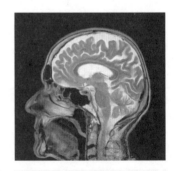

sible that the relationship between reward neurocircuitry and obesity follows the Goldilocks principle. The perversion of this faculty leads to more misery and unhappiness than almost any other thing. Using fMRI, his team scanned the brains of adolescent girls. The appetite which asks for "Rum, rum." Ratcheted down in our obesogenic world.

We may eventually be able to figure out who needs their dopamine cranked up. It exhausts the saliva.

George Combe, *Elements of Phrenology*; Luke Stoeckel, "The Goldilocks Principle or Obesity," *Scientific American Mind*; Samuel Roberts Wells, *How to Read Character: A New Illustrated Hand-book of Phrenology*; J.R. Minkel, "Appetite-Killing Hormone Negates Joy of Eating," *Scientific American Mind*; Lydia Folger Fowler, *Familiar Lessons on Phrenology: Designed for the Use of Children and Youth*.

When I put the maps side by side…

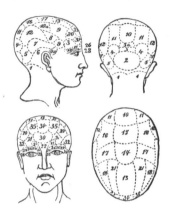 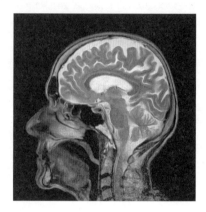

I realize the error of my own thinking, a binary pattern imposed on flow.

A winery matter deposed on dough.

A vine airy scatter reposed on snow.

the smallest interaction can change the states

In Edgar Allan Poe's "The Man of the Crowd," a familiar figure can exist only in the presence of others. Alone on the street, he turns pale, losing his life-blood. When he finds a crowded thoroughfare, "the sounds of human life" revive him. The crowd is the heart, a synergistic system of multifactorial dynamics. I stop fully in front of the wanderer, gaze at him steadfastly in the face.

An Alternative Pattern

Letter to the editor of *The New York Times*, 11/14/07, signed by
17 cognitive neuroscientists: "…we know that it is not possible to
definitively determine whether a person is anxious or feeling con-
nected simply by looking at activity in a particular brain region.
This is so because brain regions are typically engaged by many
mental states, and thus a one-to-one mapping between a brain
region and a mental state is not possible."

Whitman wrote "the pulses of your brain waiting their chance"

they seep between regions and cover the entire cortical surface
with a faint blue veneer

they swarm, flock, shoal

as crickets sync
they merge and sing in a changing cycle
femurs against forewings

aggregate choruses, temporary unisons that then move on
a glacier of fluids,
the coincidence of their calls

the pulses of the brain await their chance
as bodies of starlings in cloudstorm
form, splay, and re-form

pulled together by the simplest of rules:
don't get too close,
don't get too far from your neighbor

everyday agents sufficiently stirred by the earth's rotation
wandering stars, confined to no orbit

a pattern imposed on flow
a swarm of small causes in the tent city of neurons
protesting at the edges of cities, within private parks,
beside city halls, on campus lawns

the pulses travel the same currents
constellatory matter repositioning
the smallest interaction can change "the results of The States."

SYSTEM OF DISPLAY

The Grooved Brain Coral is named for its appearance. It looks amazingly like a human brain and has particularly deep grooves that resemble the brain's folds. In deeper waters, it can even have a grayish appearance. It is a large, reef-building coral that lives throughout the Caribbean Sea and adjacent waters. The grooves may also resemble a maze or labyrinth, giving rise to the scientific name "labryinthiformis."
—Oceana.org

...all nature is so full...
—Gilbert White

Wagner Free Institute of Science. Photograph by Joseph Elliott.
Historic American Buildings Survey.

there are general patterns

in this intertidal life

kingdom Animalia

Coral is animal, a colony of polyps dressed in algae. The algae give color, photosynthesizing the sun. Polyps have stingers, graspers, to draw the nutrients in. Then the coral exudes a skeleton, a shelter made from its own interior life.

chora is the dwelling place

life in the marine station

phylum Cnidaria, stinging cells

William Wagner was a cloth merchant's son born in 1796 in Philadelphia. As a child, walking along the Wissahickon creek, he began to collect minerals. Collecting is the first step towards naming.

the outermost layer of the earth curls over & lifts towards
the water's surface

look up through the water to the sky

class Anthozoa, flower animals

I might want to make a form that mirrors the coral's reliance on its environment. The polyps are mouths that share their homes with the algae; in exchange the algae produce food that the polyps eat. Except the polyps can't build a home to share without the food in the first place. Sharing simultaneous with just existing.

coral islands circle in the middle of the deep sea

craggy and jeweled before you

order Scleractinia, stony skeleton

Wagner wanted to be a scientist or a doctor, but his father had more lucrative plans for him. He was apprenticed to Stephen Girard, a merchant and banker, and one of the wealthiest men in the entirety of United States history. At twenty-one, Wagner was assigned the job of "supercargo," supervising sales on and off Girard's ship, the *Helvetius*; his older brother, Samuel, was aboard the ship *Rousseau*.

up from the outermost layer at particular sea level

you are just above and just below

family Faviidae or Mussidae, spheres with grooved surfaces

The polyps secrete limestone structures—corallum—that are as sol-id as walls, as intricate as cities. Reefs might seem an architecture built up from the sea floor, but their existence depends on the ceiling of the sea. We reach for the surface on the backs of our calcified dead. The nineteenth-century geologist Charles Lyell wrote in a letter, "Coral islands are the last efforts of drowning continents to lift their heads above water."

seeming a piece of land, but in fact a team of organisms

read them as evidence, the tip of the iceberg

genus Diploria once Madrepora, doubling back, inlet folds

The ship *Helvetius* was named after the French philosopher Claude Adrien Helvétius. In his book *De L'Esprit (Essays On the Mind)*, he argued that all inequalities can be traced back to unequal educational opportunities. "I am convinced that a good education would diffuse light, virtue, and consequently, happiness in society; and that the opinion, that genius and virtue are merely gifts of nature, is a great obstacle to the making any farther progress in the science of education...." In 1818, the same year William Wagner sailed on the *Helvetius*, the First School District of Pennsylvania was established.

look for proof that something happened here

a gentleman naturalist keeps a weather journal, for instance

species Cerebriformis, or brain stone

At night the polyps expand from their cells and hollows. Atoms of living jelly. I might want to make a form with tentacula that protrude and retract as if seizing and devouring. A myriad of offensive weapons contained in capsules, in a world of potential enemies. In a letter to his sister in 1834, Charles Darwin wrote "I have lately determined to work chiefly amongst the Zoophites or Coralls: it is an enormous branch of the organized world; very little known or arranged & abounding with most curious, yet simple, forms of structures."

radiata and coral theory is breath from the surface

see the labor of the coral animals in a deep and unfathomable sea

brain coral, Bahama Islands, E&H

At twenty-two, Darwin sailed as a supernumerary on board the *Beagle*, invited expressly to keep the captain company. The five-year voyage informed his book *The Structure and Distribution of Coral Reefs*. At twenty-one, Wagner was a supercargo on the *Helvetius*. The specimens he collected during his travels were foundational to the natural science school and museum that he eventually opened in his name. Which of these shells, minerals, corals, here under glass, were found while on that voyage? Super means above and beyond.

After the war of 1812, American goods were cheap and Girard's cargo was in demand. It was the "era of good feelings." The coral was booming and blooming, threatening to block the routes. In the years 1817 & 1818, William Wagner aboard the ship *Helvetius* stitched a long loop of trade:

from Charleston to Amsterdam
Amsterdam to Mauritius once Isle of France
Mauritius once Isle of France to Batavia now Jakarta
Batavia now Jakarta to Amsterdam
Amsterdam to Lisbon
Lisbon to Philadelphia
Philadelphia back to Charleston

your rice will be up to Amsterdam tomorrow if the wind holds to the westward

the supplies of Coffee in Holland will be curtailed, owing to the general scarcity of that article both in the East and West, the quantity which will be received from Java is far inferior to their former usual supplies, and the advanced price of that Bean in that Colony will most unquestionably influence the Sales in the mother Country

Sugar…the Sugar is coming in daily

"Rice," "Coffee" and "Sugar": unacknowledged metonyms for slave labor. The ship sailed from Charleston, a city with a majority enslaved population, to Amsterdam, the headquarters of the slaving Dutch West India Company, to the tropical plantations of British Mauritius (recently French Isle de France) and Dutch Batavia (now Jakarta). But the concerns of the supercargo were weather, permits, and profits. And for Wagner, the collection of specimens to build an impossibly neutral index of the world. Graspers and stingers cloak skeletons or was it the other way around?

Ship Helvetius to proceed, to Lisbon, there to take on Salt and Specie

The cargo of the Helvetius is all landed but the Iron, and am sorry to state, that after examination the cheese, Hams, & smoked Salmon, suffered considerably

As to saltpetre, little can be said as to the price, this being an article entirely depending on Peace or War

In the Prow
12 twelve casks of Beer
14 fourteen packages of cordage
318 bars & 45 bundels of Iron
35 large and small Edam cheeses

Packing the extra space in the hold with diverse sorts of drugs
Cassia, Yellow, Camphor, Bengal, Java 30, Borax, Rhubarb

300 large jars of ginger
20 small jars of ginger

We are now in sight of the Light House and going to Sea with a fine Breeze from N.W. with every Prospect of a Short Passage. I remain with Respect
Your obed. Servt.
Wm Wagner

In the museum of the Wagner Free Institute of Science, in a vertical case on the bottom shelf, is a large hemisphere of brain coral; its ridged convolutions, its labyrinthine valleys and depressions, resemble your brain. The handwritten label says "Diploria cerebriformis E&H, Bahamas, 3332." Diploria is the genus, cerebriformis the species. E&H is for Henri Milne-Edwards & Jules Haim, the first recorders of this specimen type; the Bahamas, its point of collection. The accession number, 3332, indicates that this particular specimen was added to the collection after Wagner's time. Scientific facts.

zoophyte for the mass, polyp for the individual

animals budding, but not completely separating

see their bones on the outside

Brain corals can live for up to 900 years; so it can be assumed that specimen 3332 witnessed much history before being plucked from the sea. For instance, the loyalists' retreat to the British Bahamas after the American Revolution, enslaved people working the colonized land; for instance, the people freed from foreign ships in Bahamian waters when the British outlawed the slave trade 1807; for instance, those who escaped from Florida to freedom on canoes and sloops in the early 1820s, before a new lighthouse blocked the route; for instance, the cotton picked by slaves in Charleston, shipped to the Bahamas in order to avoid the Civil War blockade; for instance, those who stowed away on those ships full of cotton in order to be free once they stepped on Bahamian soil. Bahamas from *baja mar* means shallow sea means some will swim and some will drown. Human acts.

you live on chance-bits caught with lasso cells

"a spiral array of toxic stinging barbs"

confined to the warmer regions of the globe

Warming water causes coral to expel the algae it hosts. With that, starvation and a loss of color. Low-flying planes above the Great Barrier Reef can spot the extended bleached bones in the water. I might want to make a form where a dead one comes alive. While nineteenth-century lectures on ancient coral reefs are carefully preserved in manila archival folders, twenty-first-century data on climate change is scrubbed from public view.

the brain coral has no brain

always united in a long waved series

a system of valleys with rows of mouths in several of the hot seas

When Stephen Girard died in 1831, he left none of his riches to his family and willed almost everything to the founding and endowment of Girard College, a boarding school for poor white orphan boys. Inspired by his example, Wagner devoted his later life to creating a free school where any adult could attend college-level science classes. Girard's College still provides free education to low-income Philadelphia children; after a long struggle, the school finally opened its doors in 1968 to boys of every race (and to girls in 1984). Wagner's Institute—a quarter mile northwest of Girard College—still provides free science classes, but is perhaps more recognized as a perfectly preserved example of a Victorian museum. A fossilized form of knowing.

the chorus of the coral is choral

encircled by a ring of snow white breakers

above which is the blue vault of heaven

The last coral-reef crisis was 55 million years ago. Some say the Great Barrier Reef will be extinct by 2030, possibly sooner. Black band disease, yellow band disease, white plague. I might want to make an analogy: as the skeleton protects the polyp, so does the reef protect the coast, as the glass case protects the specimen. But it doesn't work at all because the specimens are dead.

the ocean throws its breaks like an enemy

against the coral rag of the oolite

that's you there illuminated by a vertical sun

At the opening ceremonies for the Wagner Free Institute of Science in 1855, Philadelphia Mayor Robert T. Conrad compared the value of education to "the value of the vivifying sun of this bright May Morning." Twelve lectures were given a week, on geology, chemistry, anatomy, etc. The permanent building was dedicated in 1865, less than a month after Abraham Lincoln was assassinated. While the newspapers reported up to 600 students attending nightly in 1857, an 1869 entry in the annals noted a "medium audience," partially due to "the demoralized state of society, incident to the late Rebellion, precipitating upon society a large number of bad characters who carried out their crimes in private places and unlighted streets." It is the only intersection between the Institute and the tumultuous events of the day that I can find.

your meandering depressions and gothic ridges

the long swell never ceases, the consolidated debris

unconscious instruments of stupendous operations

Prof. Kirkpatrick, Lectured on Civil Engineering, at 7, Dr. Child, at 8 on the organs of Sight. He gave a most interesting lecture, illustrated by the recent eye of a Bullock, also Diagrams, weather bad, audience small.

On the radio, in defense of a new "sugary drinks" tax that pays for pre-kindergarten school programs, Philadelphia's mayor says "education is everything."

16th, Nothing Special
Dr. Child, concluded his remarks on vision etc., at 7.
Prof. Wagner, at 8, on Volcanoes, etc.

A few weeks ago, a newspaper article reports that two thirds of the Great Barrier Reef is dying or dead.

Dr. Child Lectured at 7 o'clock, on the Teeth.
Prof. Wagner, at 8, on Earthquakes.
Weather disagreeable, audience small.

When I read the local newspaper online, an ad fills up my screen urging me to tell my legislators to "ax the tax."

Dr. Child, Lectured at 7, on the Digestive organs.
Prof. Wagner, at 8, Concluded his remarks on Earthquakes, etc. Audience good but much disturbed by a noisy meeting of Druids, in the upper Hall.

Facts flex and change based on a determination of my likes and dislikes. Ice reflects the sun back into space.

I might want to see the teeming archives of the organized world, single file in the valleys of convolutions.

I might condemn empirical knowledge detached from culture.

I might become a mineralized skeleton of the lily-shaped radiaria pouring its calcareous secretion on the parent mass.

> You might claim the current climate a form of denial.

> You might be a nervous system

> Inside hemispheres with valleys that extend the entire width of domed colonies.

I might propose an expert separate from the world.

I might inhabit an intermural furrow, a double-valley character broader than the true valley.

I might register a paradigm shift in modes of understanding.

> You might be a ribbon-like columella feeding on small drifting animals.

> You might be the expert called into question.

> You might slip on the deep arm of the sea, an unexpected shelf trapped in a greenhouse gas mantle.

I might opine that these days opinion determines fact.

I might point to problems in the celestial mountains, irreversible melting flooding the ports.

I might say scientific facts are symbiotic with human acts.

                    You might reply "look up into a green sky of
                              photosynthetic bacteria."

                You might argue that science is what determines culture.

            You might be devastated by the crown-of-thorns starfish and
                cyclone scouring, succumb to warmer waters and become
                              a crumbling mound of calcium.

I might want symbiotic bargains.

I might shout that the earth can't buffer.

I might dream of a broadcast spawner that anchors in the vast aquatic deserts of open sea.

                You might hallucinate the delicate arms of a basket star
                              reaching out to predict the future.

                You might grasp and sting the brittle flower animals.

                You might want all of the surface area, all of the sun.

Sources and Acknowledgements

for "Motion Studies"

Robert Michael Brain, *The Pulse of Modernism: Physiological Aesthetics in Fin-de-Siecle Europe*, Seattle and London: University of Washington Press, 2015.

Marta Braun, *Picturing Time: The Work of Etienne-Jules Marey (1830-1904)*, Chicago and London: University of Chicago Press, 1992.

Francois Dagognet, *Etienne-Jules Marey: A Passion for the Trace*, New York: Zone Books, 1992.

Mary Ebeling, *Healthcare and Big Data: Digital Specters and Phantom Objects*, New York: Palgrave-MacMillan, 2016.

Michel Frizot, *La Chronophotographie*, Musée de Beaune, 1984.

William Kentridge, all of his work, but especially his animations and flip books.

Jill Lepore, "Not so Fast," *The New Yorker*, October 12, 2009, Pp. 114-122.

Thomas Y. Levin, Ursula Frohne, and Peter Weibel, *Ctrl [Space]: Rhetorics of Surveillance from Bentham to Big Brother*, Cambridge: MIT Press, 2002.

Stephen Mamber, "Marey, the analytic, and the digital," *Allegories of Communication*, 2006

Étienne-Jules Marey, *Animal Mechanism: A Treatise on Terrestrial and Aerial Locomotion*, New York: D. Appleton and Company, 1890.

" " , *History of Chronophotography*, from the Smithsonian report for 1901, pp. 317-340, Washington.

" " , *La Chronophotographie*, Paris: Gauthier-Villars, 1899.

" " , *Physiologie Experimentale*, Paris: G. Masson, 1880

" " , *La Méthode Graphique dans les sciences expérimentales et principalement en physiologie et en médecine*, Paris: G. Masson, 1878.

" " , *Movement*, New York: D. Appleton and Company, 1895. Reprinted by New York: Arno Press & The New York Times, 1972.

" " , *Le Vol de Oiseaux*, Paris: G. Masson, 1890.

Laura Poitras, *Astro Noise: A Survival Guide for Living Under Total Surveillance*, New York: Whitney Museum of American Art/ Yale University Press, 2016.

Anson Rabinbach, *The Human Motor: Energy, Fatigue, and the Origins of Modernity*, Berkeley: University of California Press, 1990.

Bruce Schneier, *Data and Goliath: The Hidden Battles to Collect Your Data and Control Your World*, New York: W. W. Norton & Co., 2015.

H.A. Snellen, *E.J. Marey and Cardiology*, Rotterdam: Kooyker Publications, 1980.

Hito Steyerl, *How Not to Be Seen: A Fucking Didactic Educational Mov. File*, https://www.artforum.com/video/id=51651&mode=large&page_id=14

Flip book "images" at the end of each non-fiction paragraph are from the screenplays for *Blade Runner*, *Snake Eyes*, and *Minority Report*, except for the second half of part 2, where images describe any number of films made with motion capture software.

Early versions of this project appeared in *Antennae* 11 (thanks to Jesse Seldess) and the PEN Poetry Series (thanks to Brian Blanchfield). An excerpt, translated into Portuguese by Cyriaco Lopes appeared in *Poesia Visual* 5, Oi Futuro 2017 (thanks to Lopes and Terri Witek). Additional thanks to Thalia Field, Janet Zweig, and Mary Ebeling for crucial feedback and first readings. Thanks to Hoa Nguyen for Poseidon and the two of pentacles; to the MacDowell Colony; to Temple University.

for "Popular Science"

George Combe, *Elements of Phrenology,* John Anderson Publisher, 1828.

Lydia Folger Fowler, *Familiar Lessons on Phrenology,* New York: Fowler and Wells, 1847.

O.S. and L.N. Fowler, *New Illustrated Self-Instructor in Phrenology and Physiology*, New York: Fowler and Wells, 1859.

Edgar Hungerford, "Poe and Phrenology," *American Literature*, vol. 2, no. 3 November 1931, pp. 209-231.

Kyle Kirkland, "High-Tech Brains: A History of Technology-Based Analogies and Models of Nerve and Brain Function," *Perspectives in Biology and Medicine*, vol. 45, no. 2, Spring 2002, pp. 212-223.

Nathaniel Mackey, "Phrenological Whitman," *Conjunctions* 29, Fall 1997. http://www.conjunctions.com/archives/c29-nm.htm

Edgar Allan Poe, "The Man of the Crowd," *Great Short Works of Edgar Allan Poe*, Harper & Row, 1970.

Madeleine B. Stern, *Heads & Headlines: The Phrenological Fowlers*, University of Oklahoma Press, 1971.

James Salazar, *Bodies of Reform*, New York University Press, 2011.

William R. Uttal, *The New Phrenology: The Limits of Localizing Cognitive Processes in the Brain*, MIT Press, 2001.

Samuel Robert Wells, *How to Read Character, New York and London*: Fowler and Wells Company, 1899

Walt Whitman, "Leaves of Grass: A Volume of Poems Just Published," In *Re Walt Whitman*, Horace Traubel, ed., David McKay Publisher, 1893.

And countless articles from *Scientific American Mind, Psychology Today*, and a variety of science blogs.

A version of this piece was published in *Triple Canopy* as part of the "Common Minds" series (thanks to Lucy Ives and Dawn Chan). Additional thanks to Matt Cohen, the Walt Whitman Archive, and Duke Special Collections for Whitman's phrenological report, and to Jeremy Tessiere for talking neuroscience. Thanks to Julia Foulkes and to Anna Moschovakis for helping me rethink it.

for "System of Display"

James Bowen, *The Coral Reef Era: From Discovery to Decline*, Springer Books, 2015.

Damien Cave and Justin Gillis, "Large Sections of Australia's Great Reef Are Now Dead, Scientists Find," *The New York Times*, March 15, 2017.

Thomas P. Cope, *Philadelphia Merchant: The Diary of Thomas P. Cope*, South Bend, IN: Gateway Editions, 1978.

James Dwight Dana, *Corals and Coral Islands*, New York: J. J. Little & Co., 1872.

Charles Darwin, *The Structure and Distribution of Coral Reefs*, New York: D. Appleton and Company, 1889.

Thomas M. Doerflinger, *A Vigorous Spirit of Enterprise. Merchants and Economic Development in Revolutionary Philadelphia*, University of North Carolina Press, 2012.

Elizabeth Doi, *Behind the Gates: The Wagner Free Institute of Science and its Neighborhood, 1865-Today*, University of Pennsylvania Scholarly Commons.

Emma Garman, *History of the Wagner Free Institute of Science and Its Contributions to Education*, Temple University dissertation, Department of Education, 1941.

C. A. Helvétius, *De L'Esprit; or, Essays on the Mind and Its Several Faculties*, London: M. Jones, 1807.

John Bach McMaster, *The Life and Times of Stephen Girard, Marine and Merchant*, Philadelphia: J. B. Lippincott Company, 1918.

J. E. N. Veron, *A Reef in Time: The Great Barrier Reef from Beginning to End*, Cambridge: Harvard University Press, 2008.

Matthew White, "Science for All: The Wagner Free Institute of Science," *Pennsylvania Legacies*, Vol 15, No. 1 (Spring 2015), pp. 12-17.

This piece was published in *Conjunctions 69: Being Bodies* (thanks to Bradford Morrow). It was written with the help of a Temple University-Wagner Free Institute of Science Humanities & Arts Research Fellowship (thanks to Lynn Dorwaldt and Ken Finkel). Additional thanks to Robert DuPlessis, the American Philosophical Society library, and Katherine Haas (director of Historical Resources at Girard College).

Sincere thanks to Nicholas Fuenzalida and Anna Moschovakis for their careful readings and smart suggestions. Finally, this book could not have been written without Amze Emmons, who listened to me think it through from beginning to end, and whose playful and keen observations inspire me every day.

The Dossier Series from Ugly Duckling Presse was founded in 2008. Dossier publications don't share a single genre or form—poetry, essay, criticism, interview, artist book, polemical text—but an investigative impulse, broadly conceived.

The Dossier Series includes the following titles: